American Wines

A N D

Wine-Making

BOOKS BY

Philip M. Wagner

American Wines and Wine-Making
(*1933, 1936, 1956*)

A Wine-Grower's Guide
(*1945, Revised 1965*)

These *are* BORZOI BOOKS,
Published by ALFRED A KNOPF *in New York*

American Wines

A N D

Wine-Making

by Philip M. Wagner

NEW YORK   ALFRED A. KNOPF

1974

L. C. catalog card number: 56-5436
© Alfred A. Knopf, Inc., 1956

THIS IS A BORZOI BOOK
PUBLISHED BY ALFRED A. KNOPF, INC.

First published September 1933 as AMERICAN WINES AND HOW TO MAKE THEM. Second edition, revised, with two additional chapters and a new preface, August 1936. Third edition, with the present title, rewritten and completely revised, reset, and printed from new plates, February 1956. Fourth edition, April 1961.

Fifth edition, Published December 1963
Reprinted six times
Eighth printing, March 1974

FOR

Jocelyn

Preface

In the twilight of the prohibition era, I ventured to perform a service for my fellow countrymen by writing a book entitled *American Wines and How to Make Them.* Its purpose was to lay before the domestic wine-maker the elements of the wine-making art and so to help him make good wine instead of bad out of the grapes at his disposal. There was (and still is) a dearth of sound books in the English language on wine-making. My book was published in 1933, revised once, and reprinted several times.

Much has happened in the subsequent two decades to affect the subject matter of that book. Winegrowing has re-established itself in our own country as a substantial division of agriculture, especially in California. Wines from the European districts of importance have long since returned to the American market, to pace the production of our own vineyards. Great strides have been made by œnologues in the understanding of the phenomena of fermentation and aging, with consequent improvements in wine-making methods. A whole new family of grapevines for wine-making, the so-called French hybrids, now enriches our horticulture and promises to revolutionize American winegrowing in every part of the country except California. The domestic wine-maker, producing table wines in modest quantities for the use of himself and his family, continues to flourish, but on a different basis. Now he makes wine from choice and not from necessity. Now, more often than not, he has broadened his interest to include a small vineyard, having perceived that wine can be no better than the grapes from which it is made and that the only way to assure the proper grapes is to grow them oneself, and he thus presides over the whole process from the flowering of the vines to the pulling of the cork.

So it has seemed best (a new edition being needed anyway) to replan and rewrite the book from start to finish and even to give it a new title more consistent with its altered nature.

A book of this sort is a collaboration with the dead as well as the living. Some of my dead collaborators, beginning with Cato the Censor, will be found embalmed in the bibliography. As for the living, it is quite impossible to name them all. In California, I think first of Maynard Amerine and (especially for his labor in reviewing Chapter V) Maynard Monaghan, plus Winkler, Olmo, the Ficklins, the directors and judges at several wine-judging sessions of the State Fair, and then of dozens of others. In the East, they are especially Adhemar DeChaunac, Richard Wellington, Charles Fournier, Alexander Brailow, Greyton Taylor, and the others who are banded together in a society (so far nameless) for the improvement of winegrowing; and, in Maryland, Emile J. Lussier, farmer, of Westminster, whose superbly managed vineyard has given many of the new French hybrids their first really practical test under American conditions. In France, I think first of Gerard Marot, of Poitiers, and what he has done for progress in contemporary French viticulture; then of such guardians of traditional standards in the field of the *grands vins* as the brothers Latour of Beaune, and the late Raymond Baudouin; then of the younger generation of winegrowers as personified by Lucien Lurton of Bordeaux, François Duntze of Reims, and Jean-Paul Blanck of Kientzheim in Alsace. But whether it be California, the Finger Lakes, France, or Riderwood, the one essential collaborator is my wife Jocelyn. Without her collaboration there would be no Boordy Vineyard and its wines, nor would the work of propagating and popularizing the new wine-making hybrids have been undertaken—and without those preliminary exercises the project of this book could not have been carried through.

I am grateful to the proprietors of *Guide Michelin* for permission to reproduce, with a few minor emendations, the map that appears on page 17. For the use of certain photographs I wish to thank the following: Inglenook Vineyard, Charles Krug Winery, Buena Vista Wine Co., Urbana Wine Company, Taylor Wine Company, and, for photographs of Château Pontet-Canet and Clos de Vougeot, Mr. Tom Marvel. Also, I thank my secretary, Captain Michael F. Lhotsky, for all the work he has done in putting and keeping the manuscript in shape.

PHILIP M. WAGNER

Boordy Vineyard
Riderwood, Maryland
March 31, 1955

ix

A Note on This Printing

A number of changes of detail have been made in this fourth printing of the Fifth Edition. However, Chapter V, "American Wine Today," presents a special problem. Our winegrowing industry, both Californian and Eastern, is in a state of continual and quite rapid evolution. In California there is a renewed tendency toward concentration of ownership, the most conspicuous recent cases being the absorption of the fine old independent, Inglenook, by the giant Allied Grape Growers, the absorption of Allied in turn by Heublein, and the purchase of the Almadén Vineyards by National Distillers; and Gallo absorbs an ever-increasing proportion of the total vintage. Urban sprawl continues to make inroads on important viticultural areas around San Francisco Bay and in southern California, and there has been a spectacular development of an entirely new area in the Salinas Valley with the emphasis on quality varieties. In the East, as in California, the trend toward concentration is being balanced in part by the emergence of new winegrowing enterprises. In new plantings the shift from the old grape varieties to the new French hybrids is more decided than ever, to the advantage of quality. Along with that there is a resurgence of interest in some of the more hardy *vinifera* sorts, mainly among small growers—though what this will come to is still not clear. Finally, in both California and the East the production of table wines now exceeds the production of the sweet fortified wines. In view of the rapidity of change, and because it is still accurate in outline and in essentials, I have decided to let this chapter stand for a while longer.

P.M.W.
June 1969

Contents

xi

List of Plates

xiii

List of Plates

xiv

CHAPTER I

Wine and the Vine

I t will be useful to state at the beginning what this book
is, and is not, concerned with; and for this purpose let
us go to the law of the land. The regulations governing the
operation of bonded wineries in the United States say that
wine—

> shall be deemed to be the product made from the nor-
> mal fermentation of sound, ripe grapes, without addi-
> tion or abstraction, except such as may occur in the
> usual cellar treatment . . . .

We are not going to concern ourselves, then, with such
confections as berry wine, dandelion wine, or parsnip wine.
For the purpose of this book, wine is a beverage made from
the juice of sound, ripe grapes, and nothing else. That is the
stuff the elder Pliny had in mind when he wrote, two thousand years ago, that wine "refreshes the stomach, sharpens
the appetite, blunts care and sadness, and conduces to slum-
ber." And yet that simple definition embraces great variety.
Wine may be red or white, still or sparkling, dry or sweet,
clean and fresh or rich and heady; and within each category

3

there are all sorts of variations, some obvious and some subtle, so that the use of wine is an endless adventure with something always ahead that is new and different while raising echoes of past experience. Wine does all the things that Pliny wrote of, and makes the poets sing besides.

Wines White and Red. The words *white* and *red*, as applied to wine, signify more than color. Red wines may range in hue all the way from inky purple, like the wines made from the Petite Sirah of the Rhone Valley and our Pacific coast, to the faded amber-rose of a tired but distinguished old claret; but they all have this in common: that they were fermented in intimate contact with the skin of the grape, and in the process drew from it not only color but other substances. A red wine is "solid" and "complete" in a way that white wines never are, and these vague words stand for distinct and measurable chemical and physical characteristics. White wine is something quite different. It is the juice fermented separately—in some respects a simpler thing because it lacks the substances extracted from the skin. There are white wines, like the French Muscadet, which are practically without color. Others are pale blonds. Some, as for example many of the white wines of Germany, have even a faint glint of green. So they range through the pale yellows, the shades of bright gold, of amber, of topaz, to those which are brownish either by design (like certain brown sherries) or by accident. What they have in common is not merely an absence of redness but a composition essentially different from that of red wines.

Sparkling Wines. The model of all sparkling wines is champagne, a wine associated by many with high living and low thinking and accounted by most of us a great luxury.

4

It is an effervescent wine made according to a special and exacting method from certain grapes grown in a strictly delimited area in northeastern France. In the public mind the name of champagne is associated more with the pop of the cork than with the intrinsic quality of the wine. So naturally there are many imitations, some good and some bad, not only in France but in Germany, Italy, and Soviet Russia. Some quite good sparkling wines are made in Chile, and, as we all know, sparkling wines are made in the United States, where the word *champagne* itself is allowed to appear on the label. There are great variations in the quality of the American so-called champagnes, those grown and made in New York State being on the whole (but not always) superior to those of California. None is strictly comparable to the true champagne.

Other sparkling wines, which do not pop but only bubble gently, are made in many parts of the world. They are known usually as *vins pétillants* in France, and the most popular of them is Vouvray. Much wine of this type is also made in Switzerland. In Italy there are many slightly effervescent red wines, the most popular being Lambrusco.

Fortified Wines. Of the fortified wines, the sherries of Spain and the ports of Portugal are the most celebrated, the most popular, and the most largely imitated. These are in no sense beverage wines, but should be looked upon rather as liqueurs, being always too rich in alcohol and often too sweet for unmeasured drinking. They are made by the normal fermentation of the grape; but they differ from other wines in that, during or at the conclusion of fermentation, they are fortified by the addition of grape brandy. Port and sherry are therefore not for free drinking, but are at their best at the beginning or at the end of the meal, or for casual entertaining.

Fortified wines are produced in nearly every winegrowing country. In the United States, for example, about one third of our total wine production consists of these. Australia, South Africa, and Russia produce far more fortified wine than table wine. The island of Madeira still produces the Rainwaters, Buals, and Sercials associated with its name; Sicily has its Marsala; Spain, its Alicante and Tarragona. In Italy, on the islands of the Mediterranean, and indeed in most parts of the Mediterranean region, where the climate makes for extreme sweetness in the grapes, wines of this general pattern are produced in quantity.

Then there is a group of wines that are not really wines at all. Characteristic members of this family are the mistelles of France. They are made by what is known as *mutage,* which is merely the addition of brandy or alcohol to the fresh juice in sufficient quantity to stop fermentation before it has a chance to begin. These are used mainly in the preparation of vermouths and other herb-flavored wines such as the French Byrrh, Dubonnet, Saint-Raphael, Quinquina, and so on.

Natural Still Wines. So we come to the wines that, save for these preliminary skirmishes and reconnoiters, are the subject of this book, the natural still wines. They do not sparkle, but merely glow. Such alcohol as they contain is simply and solely the result of their normal fermentation. Some few, to be sure, are sweet; [1] but their sweetness is only from the residual sugar that remains when fermentation has come to an end. Most of them are dry, which is to say

[1] Sauternes, for example.

6

that they contain no perceptible sugar. These red and white table wines comprise the bulk of the world's wine. These are the wines of which Pliny spoke. Some few are "great," but most of them are "ordinary."

Let us make a point of the *ordinary* wines. Every truly wine-drinking culture is erected upon the base of these. They are drunk daily, and without fuss. They are a part of the diet of rich and poor alike and are used naturally and unselfconsciously. They are cheap and wholesome, gently stimulating,[2] and conducive to one's physical well-being. Their dietetic properties have been studied closely and are beyond dispute. They are a source of easily assimilated energy, they can provide their share of essential minerals and vitamins, their moderate acidity plays a valuable role in the digestive process. In the wine-drinking cultures, wine stands beside and is always associated with bread—as indeed it does in the Christian symbolism. Bread and wine: flesh and blood. Strange that in this predominantly Christian country of ours one of the two elements of the Holy Communion should for a time have been declared unconstitutional!

The production of the truly "great" or fine wines is infinitesimal as compared with the bulk of the world's wine. But then, life does not consist of great occasions. For ordinary occasions, ordinary wines are best.

[2] The physiologist would call wine a mild sedative, whereas the psychologist and sociologist would call it stimulating because of its anti-inhibitory effect.

: 2 :

The history of wine is the history of the vine. Where the vine is successfully grown, there wine is usually its chief product. How closely and inevitably grape-growing is associated with wine was shown during prohibition, when at least half of California's big grape production continued to wind up as wine, not in wineries but in private cellars. How could it be otherwise? Crush grapes and they will convert themselves into wine, of a sort, no matter what you do about it.

The grapevine—more properly, the genus *Vitis*—is distributed in many species throughout the temperate parts of the world. It is the single great Eurasian species, named *Vitis vinifera* by Linnæus, that gave wine to man. Some thousands of varieties of this single species exist today, the results of many centuries of selection. Wine was made in Egypt between five thousand and six thousand years ago. Wine was being dealt in as a commodity in Mesopotamia several thousand years before Christ. From the Near East, vines of this species made their way into northern Africa and eventually into Spain. They found their way to all of the habitable islands of the Mediterranean, and established themselves all along its northern shores. It is needless to dwell on the place of honor and necessity which wine and the vine held in the successive civilizations of Greece.

The Romans derived their viticulture and their wine-making practices from Greece, though ancient Latium had its wild vines too. Œnotria, meaning "wine-land," was an early Greek name for southern Italy, later used for the

8

whole of the peninsula. The famous book on farming by
Cato the Elder, who was born in 243 B.C., deals with winegrowing in full practical detail, and is fascinating reading
today for anyone at all concerned with this art—not so
much for the differences in technique which have developed during the subsequent two thousand years as for the
substantial identity of winegrowing practice as Cato knew
it and as we know it today. Cato's specifications for the
layout of a winery are not greatly different from what will
follow in this book. His description of a wine press tallies
remarkably with the old wooden-beam presses that one
still sees occasionally in French and Italian farmsteads. He
described grape varieties that still figure largely in the
Mediterranean viticulture. His vineyard practices are still
being followed in their essentials. It is at once disconcerting
and reassuring to go back to the ancient text: disconcerting
to realize how little of novelty there really is in winegrowing, reassuring to find oneself so closely involved in a continuing tradition.

For many years the sophisticated Romans would drink
none but the famous Grecian wines, even as some Americans today prefer to drink no wine at all if they cannot
drink those of France and Germany. But in due time the
Romans developed good wines of their own, from varieties
of the vinifera species found best adapted to Roman conditions.

The viticulture of France did not stem directly, as one
might suppose, from that of the Romans. A colony of Ionian
Greeks was established at Massilia (Marseille) in 600 B.C.,
and promptly took up the cultivation of the vine. The vines
they cultivated were evidently immigrants, too, brought

by the colonists from Greece and other Mediterranean lands. The most important grape of the Rhone Valley, the grape of Hermitage and Châteauneuf-du-Pape, is called Sirah. One of its still-current synonyms, Shiraz, reveals its Persian origin. Thus French viticulture came into being not as an offshoot but as a competitor of the Roman; and at times the Romans tried to suppress it. But by the second century French and Rhenish viticulture had already been established in their main outlines.

By the fifteenth century winegrowing (always based on varieties of the same mother species, vinifera) had spread beyond Europe to the Canaries and Madeira. From then to now the diffusion has continued.

: 3 :

There are, then, many varieties of the species vinifera. But how do these differ? Why so many? How did they come into being?

A vine that does well in the rich and well-watered loam of the Rhone delta can hardly be expected to succeed in the arid chalk soils of the Champagne, and vice versa. A vine adjusted to the summer heat and mild winters of the Mediterranean basin is not at home in a Carpathian winter, and vice versa. A vine adapted to a dry climate falls prey to disease in a humid climate, and one that loves moisture has a struggle in semi-desert. There is need for a great range of varieties precisely because the range of growing-conditions under which people wish to cultivate the vine is so great. And there is need for a great range of varieties also because men do not all demand the same thing of the vine. Some want wine with small effort, and care little for quality. Others seek quality rather than quantity and will put up with difficulties in order to get it. Others are content with varying degrees of compromise between quantity and quality.

We must understand that each kind of wine owes its character first of all to the grape or combination of grapes from which it is made—to the grape far more than to the wine-maker, to the grape grown under the given conditions of soil and climate. Each great and famous wine is inescapably identified with a single variety or group of varieties: the red Burgundies with the Pinot Noir; the white Burgundies with the Chardonnay, or Pinot Blanc; the red Bordeaux with the Cabernet Sauvignon; the white Bordeaux such as Sauternes with a combination of the Sauvignon Blanc, the Sémillon, and the Muscadelle; the Rhine wines with the Riesling; the perfumed Alsatian wines with the Gewurz Traminer, and so on.

Standing just beneath these, so far as quality of wine is concerned, is a substantial group of varieties, the second best, which represent varying degrees of compromise between quality and quantity. Thus in the Bordeaux district wine of the Cabernet Sauvignon is usually associated in blends with the more productive Malbec, Verdot, and Merlot; and in the Burgundy district the Pinot Noir is blended with the more productive Meunier and Gamay. Others are the Nebbiolo and Grignolino of northern Italy, the Sirah and Grenache of the Rhone Valley of France, the Mourvèdre and Cinsaut of the French Midi and the Zinfandel of California.

There are finally the sturdy mass producers, the *cépages d'abondance,* from which the greater part of the world's ordinary wine is made. They are no less famous than the varieties mentioned, and their history is long and honorable. Such are the Aramon, the Carignane, and the Alicante Bouschet, which annually produce oceans of agreeable and quickly drunk ordinaire in southern France and Algeria, the Alicante Bouschet being grown for color and acidity, the Carignane for "firmness" and "degree," the Aramon [3] for bulk. The Alicante Bouschet and Carignane are likewise the base for mass-production wine-making in California (but not the Aramon). These mass producers have their equivalents in Spain, in Italy, in Greece, in central Europe, and indeed in all winegrowing lands.

How did they come into being? We do not know, but we can make some safe guesses. The varieties of vinifera are so many, and their qualities vary so widely, that they may well have resulted from the hybridization of several archaic "missing link" species. Each was the accidental seedling offspring of two different vines, growing near each other and thus able to mingle their pollen at blossoming time. Most of such seedlings, of course, disappeared without ever being recognized, mere weeds in a hedgerow. But now and again some particularly happy union might be discovered by an observant winegrower, and the new variety isolated and reproduced by planting cuttings. The vine grown from a cutting, rather than from a seed, comes true: it is in this way that a variety, such as, for example, the Sirah, may be propagated unchanged through thousands of years.

We may guess, then, that most of the classic varieties of

[3] The most productive variety known.

wine grape had their origin as natural seedlings discovered by chance. But there is another and perhaps equally important mechanism by which new varieties come into being, that of bud mutation. A winegrower, going through his vineyard at ripening time, notices that a vine, say, of Pinot Noir has one shoot, or cane, on which there are white grapes instead of blue—or that the fruit of one cane has ripened a good ten days ahead of the rest of the vine's crop. He marks the mutant cane and at pruning time he removes it, keeps it separate, and plants cuttings made of it. These rooted cuttings ultimately develop into whole vines that have the characteristics, not of the original vine, but of that single exceptional cane.

The point is that all these classic varieties came into being spontaneously. Of all the varieties mentioned so far, only two have a full pedigree. One is the Alsatian grape Gewurz Traminer, which was discovered in a vineyard of plain Traminer by M. Oberlin, director of the Institut Viticole in Colmar, and is now the brightest jewel in the Alsatian crown. The other is the Alicante Bouschet, product of an artificial hybridization made in the spring of 1886 between two well-known southern French varieties by Henri Bouschet. Discovery of the rest was the work of sharp-eyed grape-growers who will ever remain anonymous.

But note the reference to the Alicante Bouschet, an *artificial* hybrid. This was but the first of many relatively recent hybrids deliberately created by man. The application of hybridization to viticulture resulted from an emergency caused by the sudden appearance in European vineyards of a succession of epidemic vine diseases in the latter half of the nineteenth century. The first of these was oidium, or powdery mildew, which attacks the fruit directly. The second was caused by the phylloxera, an insect that attacks leaves and roots and eventually kills the vine. Both were introduced into Europe by accident, having been brought in on vines of wild American species imported for experiment and study. It was soon found that oidium could be controlled by chemical spray. The phylloxera proved more formidable. In 1875 the French production of wine was 2,216,258,000 gallons; four years later, in 1879, it had dropped to a pathetic 679,000,000 gallons; and the phylloxera was responsible. No way of coping directly with this insect was, or has yet been, found. But in the course of this crisis a discovery was made: [4] namely, that though the succulent roots of the vinifera vines are quickly destroyed by the phylloxera, the hard, firm roots of certain wild American species are practically immune. There began a search, a successful search, for immune American vines to serve as rootstocks on which the vines might be grafted.

But though grafting on resistant rootstocks has served the vineyards of the Old World, it is not wholly satisfactory. Grafting is expensive and laborious, and there are problems of "affinity" between certain rootstocks and certain scions. Plant-breeders have long been working, therefore, on a parallel problem: that of developing what are called "direct producers"—that is, hybrids which do not require grafting, but, grown on their roots, will resist disease yet yield fruit directly suitable for wine-making.

The first of these new "direct producers" made poor wine. But the hybridizers were on the right track. Gradually they developed varieties that combine disease-resist-

[4] By M. Laliman, of Bordeaux, in 1869.

ance with satisfactory wine quality. There exist hybrid varieties that produce wine economically, of adequate quality, and in bulk. These hybrids got their decisive test during the French period of occupation by the Germans from June 1940, through the vintage of 1944, when sulphur and copper sulphate—the then-indispensable materials for spraying—were unobtainable. Vineyards of the classic vinifera varieties suffered severely; vineyards of the hybrids came through satisfactorily. Following the war the direct producers were widely planted in the non-appellation areas of France and elsewhere in Europe, though a malevolent campaign has been mounted against them recently by traditionalists and vested interests.

These vines do not and have not been intended to replace the "noble" vinifera varieties. Theirs is the humbler role of producing good *ordinaire*. But the work of hybridization continues, the object being further improvement of wine quality. The goal now is to produce hybrids having the wine-making characteristics of, say, the Cabernet of Bordeaux, the Chardonnay of Burgundy, the Pinot Noir and the Riesling, *plus* those qualities which give the hybrids their excuse for being: hardiness, disease resistance, productivity, and so on. Some progress toward this end has been made: some of the Burdin hybrids yield wine practically indistinguishable from the wine of the Gamay Beaujolais grape when grown under identical conditions. But it is still a long way to the end of the rainbow. Ironically, more of this work is today being done in this country than in France, notably at the New York Experiment Station in Geneva, New York, and by Olmo and his associates at the University of California, Davis, California. A good reason, too: we need them more badly owing to our varied and often difficult climates.

CHAPTER II

The Wines of France

Europe is still the great winegrowing region of the world. If we want to know and understand wine, we begin best by learning something of the wines of Europe and the part they play in European life. A sort of guide for this purpose could be made, somewhat laboriously, by putting together a series of paragraphs treating one by one the wines of France, Germany, Italy, Spain, Portugal, Romania, Lower Slobbovia, etc. That would be too much of a job for me, I fear, and all too likely to degenerate into a mere catalogue. Another way would be to choose a single country and treat of its wines in rather more detail. The obvious choice for such treatment is France. Although winegrowing elsewhere has greatly reduced the importance of the export market for French wines, they are still generally available in great variety, from San Francisco to New York and from Toronto to Houston. More than half of all the wine produced in the world is made in France and the vineyards of North Africa, which are no longer politically a part of France. Moreover, and despite such particular national glories as the Rhenish wines, Spain's sherry, Portugal's port,

THE WINES OF FRANCE

The principal French wine regions and vintages.

Hungary's Tokay, and Greece's Mavrodaphne, the wines of France pretty well run the gamut. If you know the wines of France with any degree of thoroughness, you are equipped with a critical apparatus permitting you to judge the virtue of any other wine that comes your way.

Almost every part of France grows wines. But there are three regions in particular whose renown is universal. These are Bordeaux, Burgundy, and the Champagne.

Bordeaux. Along the Atlantic coast of France there is an estuary roughly comparable in size to the Delaware Bay and the Chesapeake Bay of our Atlantic coast. This is the Gironde, formed by the confluence of the Garonne and Dordogne rivers; and the port of Bordeaux, located at tide-water in a position analogous to that of Baltimore on the Chesapeake, has been the center of a great wine trade since the fourth century. If wine were produced nowhere else in France, the huge area centering upon Bordeaux would be sufficient to keep France among the great winegrowing nations of the world.

The fame of Bordeaux is based chiefly on its red wines, or clarets, which are made from a half-dozen related grape varieties and have about the same resemblance to each other as a set of musical variations has to a given theme. The Bordeaux wines differ from one another, and from year to year, yet all have a distinct family character. The most famous clarets are those from the Médoc, the strip of land that stretches along the left, or west, bank of the Gironde from the outskirts of Bordeaux about halfway to the sea. It is an area that recalls the Delaware-Maryland-Virginia peninsula lying between the Chesapeake and the Delaware estuaries on our coast: semi-oceanic in climate, with hot and humid summers and an analogous pattern of rainfall, raw winters and, thanks to the influence of the sea, a relative freedom from killing spring and autumn frosts; distinguished by sandy soil, low elevation above sea level and hence sluggish drainage and much swampy land, with a predominant cover of coarse grass and scrub pine. Despite the unpromising aspect, it is here, on the better-drained pieces of land, that the famous *crus classés*, or classed growths, are located; [1] not to mention some hundreds of *crus bourgeois* producing wines nearly as good and yet other hundreds of "artisan" and "peasant" *crus*—wines showing related characteristics, but less fine. Wines of the more famous of these *crus* are "château-bottled," which is to say: bottled at the winery. Those which have no famous name to sell are disposed of in other ways, usually in bulk to the big specialists in blended "district" wines whose cellars are located in Bordeaux itself. The least good of these ultimately reach the market as mere "Bordeaux"; the better, as "Médoc"; those better still, under the names of the communes into which the Médoc is divided, such as Saint-Estèphe, Margaux, or Saint-Julien.

Yet the Médoc produces only a fraction of the red Bordeaux wines. On the right, or east, bank of the Gironde and upriver from there stretch the vineyards of the Côtes de Blaye, Fronsac, Saint-Émilion, and Pomerol. On the left bank, upstream from Bordeaux, lies the Graves district, which produces more red wine than white, though the name Graves in many minds denotes slightly sweet white wine.

[1] The three *premiers crus* are Châteaux Margaux, Latour, and Lafite, followed by Mouton-Rothschild, which is acknowledged to be "first of the seconds," and so on down through seventy-odd seconds, thirds, fourths, and fifths (of which Château Pontet Canet is the largest and most famous).

Lying also upstream from the city and on the left bank are the communes of Barsac, Sauternes, and Bommes, from which comes the other Bordeaux specialty, the sweet dessert wines we associate with the name of Sauternes. As in the Médoc, there is here a classification of the best wines, which range in quality from the famous Château Yquem down to white wines of ordinary character. Much white wine of fair to ordinary quality also comes from the vineyards of the big triangle of land, known as Entre-Deux-Mers, which lies between the two rivers.

From the point of view of the consumer, the most comforting trait of the Bordeaux wine trade is that you get what you pay for. Bargains are rare, but so are gross deceptions. Those who seek fine wine and are willing to pay the price are not likely to go wrong, because the words *"Mise du Château"* on the label, and the brand on the cork, are guarantees that a given wine has been dealt with from vineyard to bottle-bin by the producer. Likewise those who pay ninety-nine cents for a bottle which says "Bordeaux" and nothing else get a bottle of wine worth ninety-nine cents but no more.

Burgundy. Another look at the map will indicate the Côte d'Or, in north-central France. As the Bordeaux district is essentially maritime and lowland, so the Côte d'Or, which we call Burgundy, is continental in character, lying along the slope of an abrupt escarpment that protects the vineyards from the west winds. It is a stretch of slope about forty miles long ranging in width from less than half a mile to perhaps a mile and a half, beginning just south of Dijon and extending not far south of the purely viticultural (and very beautiful) town of Beaune. Of all the winegrowing

districts in France, this is the easiest to see, since riding south
out of Dijon on Route National 74 one beholds on one's
right the whole glittering sequence of these famous winegrowing communes, with the vineyards that are named
after them: in the first group, Romanée-Conti, Richebourg,
Chambertin, Clos Vougeot; then, along the subdivision
called the Côte de Beaune, come Corton, Beaune, Pommard,
Volnay, Monthélie, and the magnificent white-wine vineyards of Meursault and Montrachet. The much-divided
vineyards stretch back from the road on the right, occupying the middle and upper slopes. Occupying lower land on
both right and left sides of the highway are vineyards producing ordinary wine.

Farther south, and up to the west behind the town of
Mâcon, on an "island" of limestone soil not greatly different from that of the Côte d'Or, is the country of Pouilly, a
white wine which, like Meursault and Montrachet, is made
of the Chardonnay grape. It is a wine that sometimes rivals
those great white Burgundies in quality, and is less expensive. But except for this "island," the soil of the Beaujolais is
fundamentally different from that of the Côte d'Or, being
granitic and hence acid in its character rather than limey—
a fact of geography which leads to a remarkable result: on
the calcareous slopes of the Côte d'Or the Pinot Noir is king
and the variety called Gamay a poor second, but here the
two find their positions exactly reversed. The Pinot Noir,
on the granitic Beaujolais soil, produces wines hardly better
than ordinary, and the Gamay produces those elegant and
fruity red wines, usually drunk fairly young, which are associated with the name of Beaujolais. The best Beaujolais
are those entitled to carry the village names of Juliénas,

Chénas, Fleurie, Romanèche, Villié-Morgon, and Brouilly. All these distinctions are of great antiquity, having been worked out by trial and error over the centuries, being now beyond dispute, and reflected in a thousand ways in the life of the beautiful countryside (and in real-estate values as well).

To complete this inspection of the Burgundy district, one must make a side trip over the hills to the northwest, to a little subdistrict that has a reputation out of all proportion to its production, the *Basse Bourgogne*, where the pale, dry, and delicately strong-tasting wines of Chablis are produced under uncertain climatic conditions from the Chardonnay grape. In the entire canton of Chablis there are just 986 hectares of vineyard; so we may conclude how frequently the name of Chablis is taken in vain.

Champagne. In the champagne district fine wine comes from vines that must put up a struggle. Soil of relatively low fertility, the danger of winter killing, the frost menace in spring and fall, excess of humidity, and a short growing season make winegrowing hazardous. The grape varieties are two: the Pinot Noir [2] and the Chardonnay. The vineyards of Pinot Noir are concentrated around the eastern and southeastern slopes of a chalky tableland called the Montagne de Reims. The Chardonnay is grown for the most part on a section a few miles to the south of the town of Epernay, on what is called the Côte de Blancs. The Pinot Noir, when quickly pressed after picking, yields a dry *white* wine of considerable body. The Chardonnay, pressed in the same way, yields a lighter and more delicate white wine.

[2] There are at least five subvarieties of Pinot Noir in the Champagne district, all differing in small particulars from the Pinot Noir of Burgundy.

After fermentation these wines are assembled and blended by the great champagne houses. Differences between the great brands, or marks, of champagne are accounted for by differences in the proportions of the various wines making up the blend.[3] Subsequently the blend, or *assemblage*, is submitted to the complicated process of bottle fermentation which in the end produces this luxurious wine. Full details of the process by which champagne is made are discussed later on.

Three Lesser Regions. Look at the map once again and you will note three other regions that are as famous in France, though not outside, as the greatest. These are Alsace, the Rhone Valley, and the valley of the Loire.

The white wines of Alsace, made chiefly of the Gewurz Traminer and the Riesling, are pressing hard on the leaders. Because this district is small, and production meager and uncertain, the Alsatians have concentrated not on bulk production but on quality. These wines are the French answer to the Rhines and Moselles of the Germans.

The Rhone Valley, from Lyon to the delta, is a much larger district, and wholly different. In this sun-baked valley the influence of the Mediterranean climate makes itself felt well into the heart of France. There is a common quality in the red wines of the Rhone Valley all the way from those of the Côte Rotie and Condrieu, just below Lyon, down to the wines of Châteauneuf-du-Pape, grown near the city of Avignon. These are heavy-bodied and formidable wines, high in alcohol, rough when young, firm and round when

[3] There are a few producers, co-operatives and individual wine-growers, which specialize in "straight" or unblended champagnes. These usually carry the indication "*blanc de blanc*," meaning white wine from white grapes, or "*blanc de noirs*," meaning white wine from black grapes.

mature. Most of these Rhone wines are best classed as "superior" rather than fine. They have obvious counterparts among some of the best California red wines.

The third of this trio of lesser regions, the valley of the Loire, is a gangling area spreading all the way from Nantes (where the Loire meets the Atlantic) upstream into the Massif Central. Although a good deal of red wine is grown for local use, this is essentially a region of light and inexpensive white wines, which are bottled young and are appreciated by the French for their freshness, fruitiness, and tartness. There are certain exceptions. Not far from the city of Saumur is a pocket of red-wine vineyards producing the spicy and delicious wines called Chinon and Bourgueil. In the best years, to state the other big exception, the wines of the three subdistricts of Anjou, Coteau de Layon and Vouvray may wind up not light and tart but rich and sweet with several degrees of sugar. But on the whole these wines of the Loire and its tributary valleys carry out the generalized description: fresh, fruity, and tart. For memory, the principal wine types, working upstream from the region around Nantes, are those known as Muscadet, Anjou (with Coteau de Layon), Saumur, Vouvray, Sancerre, Chavignol, and Pouilly-sur-Loire. Every Frenchman knows these; we Americans must go to France to find them and learn how gracefully they fit into the French notion of the good life.

The Midi. So we come finally to what French specialists in such matters call the region of monoculture. All of the six regions so far mentioned—Bordeaux, Burgundy, Champagne, Alsace, Rhone, Loire—are regions of mixed agriculture in which winegrowing plays an important and often dominant part, but in which there are other important agricultural resources. This is true in the Beaujolais: the big co-operative dairy just north of Mâcon is larger than any two wineries in the whole region. In Alsace the sugar beet is as important as the vine. It is true even of Bordeaux. For though there is an intense concentration of winegrowing in the Médoc, one nevertheless may hear cows mooing among the châteaux. Winegrowing here is but one element in the pattern, allowing the prudent producer to spread his risks and also, when combined with dairying, to keep his vine-yards well manured. But in the Midi, which is to say in Mediterranean France, one encounters an utterly different situation. Here, in a half-dozen departments, the grapevine is absolutely dominant. For mile after mile along the Medi-terranean coast from Spain to the swamps and oil refineries around Marseille, the vineyards seem almost continuous. All else is subordinated to them. To the casual visitor, there seems no particular difference between one part of this dis-trict and another; yet there are important distinctions and numerous well-recognized regions. Most of the production is of extremely ordinary quality, made of the Carignane, the Alicante Bouschet, and the Aramon grape, and blended to a predetermined standard along with wines of similar type (but usually richer in alcohol and deeper in color) brought over from Algeria in tank ships. There is also wine of dis-tinctly superior quality in the Midi, produced on the high-lands and hillsides, most of them lying fairly well back from the coast. Such are the wines known as Corbières and Miner-vois and Roussillon and Banyuls, not to mention the Mus-cats of Rivesaltes, Lunel, and Frontignan, and the heavy-bodied white wine of the Picpoul grape, excellent of its type, which ultimately becomes vermouth. Such a highly industrialized viticulture has its weak points as well as its strong points, its vulnerability to overproduction and other economic ills, its vulnerability to epidemic vine diseases and to soil exhaustion, its tendency to substitute the ideal of standardization (sameness is another word for it) for the ideal of individuality. It is nevertheless the source of the urban workingman's daily wine—that is, of the wine that goes with his daily bread.

In these paragraphs of description, and on the map that accompanies them, there is room only for those wines which are truly, in the minds of most Frenchmen, among the greatest glories of French civilization. What has not been sufficiently exposed, perhaps, is the extent and infinite variety of the viticulture lying between the great regions: the vineyards that show up surprisingly, to produce a delightful pale pink wine, called *vin gris*, in the midst of Lorraine's coal and iron country, other vineyards in Poitou, high in the Savoy Alps, on steep hillsides along rushing streams in the Juras, tucked away on favorable patches of ground in the upper reaches of the valley of the Dordogne and elsewhere in the lofty and forbidding Massif Central of France. Nor can description give any notion of the number of these "little" wines, grown for village use, or simply for the family. Scratch a Frenchman in most parts of France and you expose a vigneron. A Frenchman wrote a book not long ago called *La Civilisation de la vigne*. It was an apt title: its synonym is France. Other countries produce much wine, both fine and ordinary; but nowhere else is there such variety, and nowhere else have wine and the vine so permeated the history and entered into the way of life of a people. If one knows the wines of France, one knows wine.

CHAPTER III

Our Vinous Endowment

M ore than half of the known species of *Vitis* are natives of North America; and early comers from
Europe—the explorers and settlers—were impressed as
much by the prevalence of the wild grapevine as by any
other aspect of the new land. The Norse name for America
was Vinland. Amadas and Barlow,[1] who visited what is
now Roanoke Island in 1584, reported a land "so full of
grapes as the very beating and surge of the sea overflowed
them. . . . In all the world the like abundance is not to be
found." Captain John Smith, writing in 1606, was more
specific. He mentioned two different kinds of grape: "Of
vines great abundance in many parts that climbe the toppes
of highest trees in some places, but these beare but few
grapes. Except by the rivers and savage habitations, where
they are not overshadowed from the sunne, they are covered with fruit, though never pruined nor manured. Of
those hedge grapes we made neere twentie gallons of wine,
which was like our French Brittish wine, but certainely
they would prove good were they well manured. There is

[1] Quoted by Hedrick in his classic *The Grapes of New York*.

another sort of grape neere as great as a Cherry, this they [the Indians] call *Messamins*, they be fatte, and the juyce thicke. Neither doth the taste so well please when they are made in wine." These Messamins were undoubtedly the Muscadines, the best known contemporary variety of which is the Scuppernong.

So these early comers anticipated a bright future for viticulture; and a browse through the records of our colonial history turns up a long series not only of reflections on viticultural possibilities but of ambitious projects. As early as July 1616 Lord Delaware had reported on the possibilities to the London Company, which obliged by sending over some French vignerons, together with cuttings of the best European varieties. This effort to establish a Virginia viticulture failed. The matter was approached from another direction: a law was passed requiring each householder to plant and care for a certain number of cuttings. This was no more successful. Then premiums were offered for successful cultivation. Still no wine—or so little that no one bothered to remark upon it.

Other efforts, as fruitless, were being made in every colony. In 1629, at the urging of the Governor, European grapes were planted in the Massachusetts colony; and Charles II himself arranged to have them planted in Rhode Island. The Huguenots brought the European vine to the Carolinas, with no better success. A viticultural effort in Georgia was based on cuttings from Portugal. In New Sweden, on the Delaware, the Swedish Queen encouraged an effort to establish a winegrowing industry and so free Sweden from dependence on European sources of wine. This was a serious effort, but it came to nothing. The Dutch in New Netherland had much the same experience. A traveler reported in 1679 that the Dutch enterprise had failed and that the colonists "have not as yet discovered the cause of the failure." When the English took over New Netherland, they tried too, and with no better success.

So these disappointments succeeded one another for more than two centuries. All sorts of reasons except the right one were put forward to explain the failures. The vignerons proved to be lazy, or were scalped, or ran away; a more attractive crop, like tobacco, lured the proprietor; or the vine-growers merely lost interest. What happened in fact, in every case, was that "a sickness took hold of the vines," a sickness the growers could not account for, which left them helpless. A fallacy lay behind all these early efforts: namely, that the wine grapes of Europe must surely thrive where wild grapes were so abundant. What the colonists could not know was that these wild vines were immune or nearly so to the ravages of certain indigenous pests and diseases to which the European vine was woefully susceptible. Had the colonists bent their efforts to taming the wild natives, instead of coddling the exotics from Europe, the course of American viticulture might have been different.

This was dimly perceived by some of the shrewder colonists. We have already seen that Captain John Smith went so far as to make wine of the native grapes. William Penn likewise suspected that the right course was to work with the native grapes. As early as 1683 he was suggesting that it might be better "to fall to Fining the Fruits of the Country, especially the Grape, by the care and skill of Art" than to send for "foreign Stems and Sets." He expressed the intention, "if God give me Life, to try both, and hope the consequence will be as good Wine as any European Countries of the same Lattitude do yield." Some wine was made of native grapes by the French in Louisiana. In the South along the Atlantic coast there grew up also a modest local trade in the wines of the Muscadines, or Messamins. But it is not hard to understand why these experiments were, relatively, so few and so tentative. Our native grapes are different from those of the Old World, not merely in the structure of their roots and vines, which makes them more hardy and disease-resistant, but in the qualities of the fruit. The wild American kinds, such as *Vitis labrusca* (the fox grape of the Northeast), and the Appalachian *V. æstivalis* and *V. riparia*, and the Muscadines, contain much less sugar and much more acid than the European, and they are different in appearance, texture, flavor, and smell. The "foxiness" of our most conspicuous wild species, *V. labrusca*, has always been the great stumbling-block to American wine-making. Some means of tempering the wildness of our wild grapes had to be discovered before they could become truly suitable for wine-making.

: 2 :

The first real impetus to the domestication of the native grapes was accidental. A Swiss named Jean Dufour organized, toward the end of the eighteenth century, the Kentucky Vineyard Society, to grow European grapes on a large tract in Kentucky. His enterprise failed, like its predecessors elsewhere. His vines were seized with the inexplicable "sickness," all except one variety, a black grape, which throve. This grape he had secured from one Peter Legaux, a Frenchman who had tried his hand at viticulture (without success, of course) near Philadelphia and who supposed it to be a variety that had been imported as seed from the vinifera vineyards of the Cape of Good Hope. It was known by the names of Alexander or Cape, and later by many other names, such as Vevay, Clifton's Constantia, Schuylkill Muscadel. The news of this grape spread rapidly. Dufour removed from Kentucky to Indiana and once more planted the varieties of vinifera; again the only one to survive was the Alexander. On the strength of this double success, the Alexander was widely planted, and nearly everywhere it throve. But before long certain iconoclasts were suggesting that it was not a European variety at all, but a bastard American that had fallen accidentally among its highborn cousins. Dufour denied this hotly and fought to "save its character." He died fighting, convinced to the end that he had established the European grape on American soil. Yet there is now little doubt as to the genesis of the Alexander. It was found originally by John Alexander, gardener to Governor John Penn, in whose garden he planted it. As its source was very close to a vineyard in which certain European varieties were being tried (as usual, without success), it was almost certainly an accidental cross between the wild *V. labrusca* and one of the European vines. Its flavor is that of the *labrusca;* its oval shape could have come only from a European parent. The Alexander is merely a piece of viticultural history now, for better kinds have displaced it. But it served its purpose: it made the native grape respectable.

Thanks to the Alexander, the direction of American viticulture was turned toward the native vines. Prince, the author of the first genuine treatise on American vine culture, concluded that the only sensible course was to cultivate the native species. John Adlum, writing in 1809, remarked in connection with the Alexander: "I think it would be well to push the culture of that grape without losing time and efforts in search of foreign vines." But in one sense this change came too late. Nearly two hundred years had been frittered away in fruitless, if well-meant, experiment; and during that time the opportunity to make of the American nation a wine-drinking people had been temporarily lost.

The success of the Alexander was followed quite soon by the appearance of two other natives, the Isabella and the Catawba. The Isabella need not deter us long, for its cultivation, though important for a time, has languished. It is of unknown origin, was introduced around 1816, and gained considerable popularity because of the fact that it ripened somewhat earlier than the Alexander and consequently could be grown in colder latitudes. It is still grown a little in New York State. Oddly, it is encountered occasionally in the more backward areas of Europe, where it was introduced during the phylloxera epidemic. In the southern Alps the peasants call its wine *Americano*, as distinct from *Nostrano*, the wines of better quality.

The appearance of the Catawba was more important, and for years this variety was the principal cultivated American wine grape. Its precise origin, like that of the Alexander and the Isabella, is cloudy. Hedrick says that it made its debut in 1823, in the garden of John Adlum, in the District of Columbia; and Major Adlum said that he secured the cuttings from a Mrs. Scholl, of Montgomery County, Maryland. The Scholls had always called this grape Catawba; but Mrs. Scholl's father, to the great loss of science, died before anyone thought to ask him where he got it. The late T. V. Munson said that it was found wild in the woods near the Catawba River, North Carolina, in 1801, but he gives no evidence to support his statement. In any case its wine was admired.[2] Major Adlum, a man never guilty of modesty, wrote: "In bringing this grape into public notice, I have rendered my country a greater service than I could have done had I paid off the national debt." The first Nicholas Longworth planted it in his vineyards near Cincinnati in 1825; in return the Catawba established the fame and fortune of the house of Longworth. Catawba wines held popularity right up to prohibition.

Within a decade of the introduction of the Catawba— that is, by 1830—grape culture had become a modest but commercially profitable industry. Several other varieties had also been introduced and had achieved a certain popularity. In Virginia and the Carolinas a seedling of the wild *V. æstivalis* known as Norton was being cultivated to a slight extent. In the South also the Muscadines were domesticated. The grapes of this latter family are grown on vines which assume huge proportions, spreading sometimes over many thousands of square feet and supported by trunks many feet in circumference—the banyan trees of viticulture. There are many "original" Scuppernong vines. One of

---

[2] Even by the poet. See Longfellow's dreadful verse about Catawba wine, the one which goes:

> *Very good in its way*
> *Is the Verzenay,*
> *Or the Sillery soft and creamy;*
> *But Catawba wine*
> *Has a taste more divine,*
> *More dulcet, delicious, and dreamy. . . .*

these stands on Roanoke Island; another, thought to have been found by a member of Sir Walter Raleigh's colony in 1584, was still standing on an island in the Scuppernong River, North Carolina, not so many years ago. It was originally supported by a tree, which died and rotted away, leaving the vine to stand on its own huge trunk. In the North, wherever the Catawba could not be relied upon to come to maturity regularly, the Isabella was grown. The Clinton, a cultivated variety of *V. riparia*, and the parent of many subsequent red-wine hybrids, was making way slowly.

Grape-growing steadily expanded during the two decades following the introduction of the Catawba, so that by 1850 there were prosperous vineyards in the Ohio River valley, in central New Jersey, in the Hudson River valley, along the south shore of Lake Erie around Cleveland, in certain parts of the Carolinas, and in a part of Missouri around the town of Hermann. This last district earned considerable renown subsequently for a whole series of wine grapes, developed from species indigenous to that region, of which the most famous was perhaps the Missouri Riesling, a white-wine grape. The Chautauqua and Finger Lake districts of New York State—the latter of which has always yielded our best sparkling wines—were under development. Deacon Elijah Fay had established vineyards in the first of these, and the Reverend William Bostwick was the pioneering grower in the latter, thus carrying along the traditional affiliation between Church and vine.[3]

[3] Deacon Fay was a Methodist; the Reverend Mr. Bostwick an Episcopalian.

: 3 :

Then in 1852 occurred a great pivotal event in the history of American grape culture: the Concord appeared on the scene. Its introduction was important mainly because it turned the attention of grape-growers away from wine and toward the table. The fated seed from which the Concord was to spring was planted in 1843 by one Ephraim Bull, of Concord, Massachusetts. The vine came to bearing several years later, and the fruit was exhibited before the Massachusetts Horticultural Society in the year 1852. The Concord was an instant success. Not only was its fruit attractive and agreeable to eat; the vine was hardy and productive and would tolerate neglect. It did well in the kitchen garden and as a commercial table grape. It proved ideal for the manufacture of unfermented grape juice. But its strongly foxy aroma makes it unsuitable for dry table wines. A monument stands at the site of the original vine, but the winemaker approaches that shrine with mingled emotions.

The Concord, to give it credit, was important in another way. Mr. Bull believed it to be a cross between the wild fox-grape and the Catawba. Whether he was right or wrong, the possibilities of developing new types by crossing were nevertheless well advertised. In the two decades that followed, fruit-growers went hybrid-mad. New varieties were produced by the hundreds. Most were worthless, but the period yielded several that are still in the front rank of our native wine grapes. Among the second- and third-generation hybrids there were some particularly fine fruits.

The greatest of these was the Delaware, named after the town of Delaware, Ohio, and not after the Lord Delaware to whom we have already made obeisance, nor yet after the state of that name. Its fruit and the bunches are small and delicately formed, pale rose in color, with a bloom of grayish lavender. It is by general agreement the best of our native white-wine grapes. Two hybridizers, E. S. Rogers, of Salem, Massachusetts, and Jacob Moore, of Brighton, New York, were quite successful. Rogers was fascinated by the possibilities of improving our wild vines by marrying them with vinifera, and from a life of experiment he gave to the world some forty varieties, which are known collectively as Rogers's Seedlings. All of these have defects that have kept them from general cultivation. Yet he is a great figure in American viticulture. Moore gave better grapes to the world than Rogers. His two best were probably Brighton, a red grape, and Diamond, a white. But even these are little grown today.

During this period also the American grapes made their famous expedition of mercy to France. When the seriousness of the phylloxera plague was realized, the European demand for American vines became very great. The French hoped to use these American varieties as "direct producers" to displace their own. They planted one called Noah, for white wine; Jacquez, a variety from *V. bourquiniana*, known sometimes as the *southern æstivalis*, which is still grown for red wine in some parts of France; Clinton, for red wine; and Othello, a hybrid of Clinton and a vinifera variety. All of these resisted the oidium and the phylloxera, and the red wines were rich in color and of sufficient alcohol and acidity. But they all had in varying degree that foxy

Chateau Pontet Canet in the Médoc.

Clos de Vougeot in the Burgundy district.

Charles Krug Winery near St. Helena, Napa Valley, California.

Count/Colonel Agoston Haraszthy.
(Courtesy Buena Vista Vineyard)

Original Buena Vista (Haraszthy) Winery, photograph taken 1865.

aroma which the French so abhor in American grapes, and the calcareous soils of Europe appear to intensify this aroma. When the possibilities of grafting were discovered, these direct producers were for the most part abandoned, or cut to the roots and used as grafting stocks *in situ,* and the French were thus enabled to return to their traditional varieties. But this European relief work was only incidental to our viticultural history. The notion of growing European vines in the Eastern United States was abandoned by practically everyone once California viticulture began to compete with that of the East. In California, with its Mediterranean climate, the European wine varieties thrive. By 1880 the shipments of California wines to the East had reached such proportions as seriously to menace the Eastern wine-making industry, and before long California was growing about eighty-five per cent of all our grapes, a proportion it has continued to maintain with only slight fluctuations.

: 4 :

Although Eastern winegrowing was thus narrowed, Eastern wine-making was by no means finished. The cultivation of our native grapes continued, in fact, to increase, though at a more moderate rate after California came into its own. By the turn of the century there were several hundred thousand acres of "Eastern" vineyards. The Chautauqua and Finger Lake districts of New York had continued to enlarge their acreage, and the Niagara peninsula district had been added. The region around Cincinnati had declined, but the northern part of Ohio along Lake Erie had heavy acreage, as did the Lake Erie islands. There were considerable winegrowing districts in Pennsylvania, Michigan, Illinois, Indiana, Kansas, Missouri, Arkansas (the Ozarks), Oklahoma, Georgia, the Carolinas, and Virginia. The central part of New Jersey, around Egg Harbor, was also producing some wines.

These wines of New York and Ohio, of the Ozarks and Virginia and New Jersey and the scattered lesser districts, were like no wines ever before known. They had their source in the peculiarly American fruits, the Catawba and the Delaware, the Niagara, the Clinton, the Missouri Riesling, the Elvira, Cynthiana, Isabella, Ives, Eumelan—and the Concord. They offered a new range of aromas and flavors, as American as doughnuts and corn on the cob. It cannot be said that many of them suited persons who had formed their taste on the wines of Europe. But they had— and will always have—their devoted clientele. They were not imitative; and for many that will always be a point in their favor.

This was the situation, then, when prohibition abruptly strangled the three-hundred-year effort in the eastern parts of the United States to realize the promise of the wild vines. We shall see what has happened since the end of prohibition. But before looking at the present state and future prospects of winegrowing in America, let us first examine the very different story of California's viticultural development.

CHAPTER IV

Concerning California

C alifornia has what the geographers call a "Mediterranean," or two-season, climate in which the rainfall
is concentrated in the mild winter months. Its Mediterranean character can be shown by numerous analogies of
temperature, rainfall, and humidity with stations in France,
Italy, Spain, and Algeria. The vinifera grapes, so much at
home in the Mediterranean basin, find California conditions
congenial. California wines have a kinship with Mediterranean wines.

There is one important difference between viticultural
California and the Mediterranean area. The latter is east-
west in orientation and borders an inland sea, whereas viticultural California is a north-south region bordering an
ocean. This produces variants of the "Mediterranean" type
of climate which the Mediterranean itself knows nothing
of. So do the enormous range of altitudes in California and
the presence of that arid but enormously fertile inland basin
known as the Central Valley.

The coast counties yield California's best dry wines, red
and white. These counties have San Francisco Bay as their

hub and stretch out to the north and south of it. The general rule is that those counties running directly into the bay produce the best wines. The three exceptions are Marin County, just north of the Golden Gate, and San Francisco and San Mateo counties, all three of which are too cool. The best wines have always come from Sonoma, Napa, and Alameda counties, with Santa Clara and San Benito pushing them closely. As grown in these counties, the red wines made of the Cabernet, the white wines made of the Chardonnay and Pinot Blanc, and some of the wines of the Sauternes type are the best wines in the European style that the United States has so far produced.

The vineyards of the coast counties have always been small as compared with those of the Central Valley. This, lying between the coastal ranges and the Sierras, is divided into the Sacramento Valley at the north, the San Joaquin Valley at the south, and the Central Valley proper in between. It is the greatest raisin-producing region of the world, and the leading table-grape region of the United States. Here, especially in the San Joaquin Valley, thousands upon thousands of acres are given over to the Muscat of Alexandria, the grape from which Muscat raisins are made, which also yields a rather coarse and highly alcoholic muscatel wine. The San Joaquin Valley is also the principal growing-region for the Sultanina, or Thompson's Seedless, from which seedless raisins are made. The Sultanina is also a table grape, and when in surplus it goes to the wineries. As a triple-purpose grape it is a comfort to grape farmers, but an ever-present threat of overproduction and lowered quality to the wine industry. There is little rainfall in the San Joaquin, and not many years ago it was a baking desert; but under irrigation its rich soil is enormously productive. Unfortunately, desert heat, irrigation, and the production of fine wines do not go hand in hand. In the Central Valley around Lodi the dominating grape is the familiar red Tokay, a table grape that is not the true Tokay grape of Hungary (which is called the Furmint), but an Arabian grape named Ahmar abu Ahmar, "Red, Father of Red." Culls usually go to the wineries and drag down quality.

In this inland valley large quantities of the more prolific wine varieties are also grown, chiefly for cheap port and sherry, but also for table wines. Soil and climate are suited to the growing of such varieties as have been cultivated for years in the south of France and in Algeria.

To the south, around Los Angeles, lies California's third viticultural region. In general this district is less appropriate for good dry wines than for sweet fortified wines.

: 2 :

It was in this southern region that California's first vines were planted. Vines and cuttings are known to have been brought from Spain as early as 1524, when Cortez was Governor of Mexico. They did well enough in Mexico, under the care of the padres; and as the line of missions advanced, the wine grape went along. In 1697 the Mission of Loreto was established on the peninsula of Lower California, and this was followed by others, until a chain of missions extended the whole length of the peninsula. The first vineyard in California proper was that of the Mission of San Diego, founded in 1769; the next earliest, that of San Gabriel, in 1771. Other vineyards followed, until the chain had reached well north of the present San Francisco. For some reason, these missions had but one grape, which not unnaturally came to be known as the Mission. The origin of the Mission is unknown; but its persistence (it is still grown a good deal) is adequately explained by its vigor, its fruitfulness, and its dependability. Many sorts yield better wine, but none are more dependable; and we may thank the Mission for the fact that there has been a vintage, of a sort, in California every year for more than a century and a half.

The Franciscans were thus the first winegrowers of California, and they were the only ones for years. It was not until 1833, when Mexico secularized the landholdings of the missions, that commercial winegrowing had a chance in California. The first of the truly commercial California winegrowers was a Frenchman, aptly named Jean Louis Vignes. Vignes knew winegrowing and the art of distillation, and shortly after his arrival in California, in 1829, he established a vineyard on the site of what is now the Los Angeles Union Station. Vignes was able to import some cuttings and was thus not entirely dependent on the Mission variety. As he was a cooper by trade, he could make casks of the native oaks. The lack of cooperage had handicapped the missions. Vignes, who came to be known as Don Luis, made a very good thing out of his enterprise and became a leading citizen. Not long after, there arrived another Frenchman, Pierre Sansevain, who went into business with him. One William Wolfskill, a trapper of beavers, turned to the grape and contributed the element of competition to the growing industry, likewise establishing himself on land that is now part of downtown Los Angeles.

These men were well established by the end of the 1830's. But American settlers did not begin to arrive in California in considerable numbers until the forties. Most of these were gold-seekers, yet among them were some few who had the wit to see the possibilities of the land itself. One of these was a remarkable Hungarian, Count Ágoston Haraszthy de Mokcsa, who almost singlehanded planted the seeds of California's present-day viticultural industry. Haraszthy was a member of the minor Hungarian nobility, a native of Futtak, then a provincial Hungarian town, now a part of Yugoslavia. An army officer and an important civil servant, he nevertheless had small regard for monarchical institutions. This damned him in the eyes of the higher authorities and compelled him finally to flee his country in disguise. After preliminary wanderings he came finally to America in the spring of 1840, choosing Sauk City, Wisconsin, as the place to establish himself. The impact of Haraszthy on Sauk City was immediate and lasting. To say that he ran things in that region would be to err on the side of understatement. But Sauk City failed to hold him; and by 1850 he had transplanted himself and his progeny (his three sons were named Gaza, Attila, and Arpad) to San Diego, then a wild frontier village. In San Diego he made as strong an impression as he had in Sauk City. Within a year he was appointed sheriff and set about subduing the Indians. In 1852 he was elected to California's General Assembly, in which body he promptly made himself a commanding figure. But though he represented San Diego ably for his term, he never returned there to live; his attention was diverted to San Mateo County. It was then, apparently, that he began to meditate seriously upon California's viticultural possibilities; and soon he had arranged for the importation of a collection of vines from Europe. Among those he received was the Alexandria (Muscat of Alexandria), and he must therefore be accounted the father of California's present raisin industry. Then he received a half-dozen varieties from Hungary. Just what they were is now lost to the record, but it seems probable that one of them was the Zinfandel, which in a comparatively short time ousted the Mission as the staple variety. There is no grape called Zinfandel in Hungary; how the name originated is anybody's guess.

But Colonel Haraszthy (somewhere between Sauk City and California he ceased to be Count and became Colonel) soon realized that San Mateo County is not ideal for grapes, and in 1856 he acquired a tract in the Sonoma Valley, whither he removed his wife, his increasingly numerous offspring, his father, the mild and scholarly "Old General," and his effects. The discovery that the best of the Franciscan wines had come from Sonoma doubtless had some influence on his choice. Within two years he had a vineyard of 85,500 vines and a nursery of 460,000 rooted cuttings. He distributed cuttings and vines lavishly, and from this first large-scale distribution by Haraszthy certain varieties emerged which have since become staples of California viticulture, among them Flame Tokay, Emperor, Riesling, Traminer. He also lectured and addressed papers to agricultural societies. He had much inertia to overcome. The report of the U.S. Patent Office for 1856 (this was the predecessor of the Department of Agriculture), though it treats of grapes and wine-making at great length, makes no mention whatever of California. But Haraszthy succeeded in attracting the interest of a number of men whose names were to become bywords in California winegrowing: Charles Krug, Jacob R. Snyder, Emil Dresel, Jacob Gundlach, and others. In 1861 he persuaded the state to establish a Viticultural Commission and appoint him chairman. Armed with his title, and at his own expense, he set forth with his sons Attila and Arpad upon a viticultural tour of Europe.

The Colonel returned with a heightened opinion of California; also he brought two hundred thousand vines and cuttings, included among which were all the most important varieties of Europe. These he put in nursery, then distributed them for trial. There is no doubt that in his enthusiasm he mixed a good many labels and made mistakes. Yet in little more than a decade his efforts did endow California with the results of two thousand years of European grape-growing. Having done this, he disappeared from the scene almost as suddenly as he had appeared. The ambitious wine-making enterprise he founded was a commercial failure. Haraszthy had no head for business.

: 3 :

As a result of the Haraszthian inspiration, there was a spurt in California wine-making. The first *Annual Report* of the Department of Agriculture, published in the year 1862 and addressed to Abraham Lincoln, makes recognition of this by devoting several pages to California's winegrowing possibilities. The state's yield of grapes and wine increased steadily. By 1877 the vintage had reached the considerable bulk of four million gallons. But most of the early wine-growers, though they shared Haraszthy's enthusiasm, did not share his sound intuitions. They did not heed his caution to make haste slowly. The result was much wine of an inferior sort, and an industry that soon became notorious for slipshod practices.

Having thus earned a bad name for themselves, the Californians [1] then compounded it by perpetrating a variety of frauds and near-frauds—adulteration, misbranding, and the like. Conditions became so nearly intolerable that finally the better winegrowers banded together and in 1880 got the state legislature to pass a Pure Wine Law, with teeth, to end the grosser types of fraud. This law had its positive as well as its negative or regulatory purpose. Its title, "An Act for the *Promotion* of the Viticultural Interests of the State," indicates as much; and accordingly a State Board of Viticulture was set up for the dissemination of reliable information on viticulture, wine-making, cellar management, and trade practices. The University of California, also, was directed to undertake investigation and instruction in the technical aspects of the art.

The law swiftly eliminated the worst abuses, and the Board of Viticulture and the university did useful extension work. True, the board, representing the commercial interests, and the university, representing the disinterested viewpoint, were much given to feuding. Yet both were in fact working toward the same end: the improvement of

[1] Always excepting an enlightened and conscientious minority that appreciated the importance of building a sound reputation on sound wine and worked unceasingly to that end.

California's wines.[2] Under the law, and with the co-operation of a sufficient number of growers and wineries, the great Professor E. W. Hilgard was able to direct investigations into many aspects of winegrowing, especially the peculiar problems of wine-making in hot climates. If Haraszthy founded this industry, Professor Hilgard and those who worked with him established it on a solid basis. In consequence of this work many California wineries became models of up-to-date practice. The California wines, freed of their taint, began to offer stiff competition in the Eastern markets to the products of the wine-makers of New York, Ohio, and Virginia, who were working with native grapes, and also to imported wines.

During the era of reform which was inaugurated by the Act of 1880 the outline of California's viticulture began to be filled in and the advantages and limitations of each district to be understood. It was more and more evident that the best of the dry wines would come from the coast counties, and there certain vineyards began to stand out as definitely superior. The practice of estate bottling—which is the surest proof of pride in the making and good faith in the selling of wine—was adopted by the proprietors of many of these better vineyards. Between 1877 and 1895 production jumped from 4,000,000 gallons to 17,000,000 gallons. A good deal of this wine never left the state— California has always been the largest wine market in the United States—but shipments to the East kept on growing, and there even developed a modest export trade. There

[2] It is pleasant to record, also, that since the repeal of prohibition the university and the contemporary trade organizations, the Wine Institute and the Wine Advisory Board, have been farsighted enough to work in harmony.

47

were tentative, if not sensationally successful, efforts to break into the European market.

The Californians were beginning to discover, in the meantime, that they had another enemy to fight besides their early reputation. That was the phylloxera. No one knows precisely when or how this native of the East got over the mountains. But it got there, and it was greeted as it had been in Europe. First it mystified, then it was dismissed as a passing blight, then it was fought with oratory and indignation, and finally it aroused something approaching panic. But the panic never reached the intensity that it reached in Europe, for the phylloxera has never worked its destruction so rapidly in California.

Because the phylloxera spread slowly, the fight against it (by grafting, as in Europe) could be launched in sufficient time to save the industry from calamity. But the counterattack against the phylloxera had no sooner been mounted than a major diversion appeared in the neighborhood of Anaheim, a big grape-growing center of that time lying south and east of Los Angeles. The Anaheim district had had its beginning as a quasi-religious co-operative venture back in the fifties.[3] But piety did not keep the symptoms of a mysterious new disease from appearing suddenly in the 1880's in these vineyards. It was not the phylloxera, nor could its identity be established; nor was any satisfactory treatment discovered. It was swiftly fatal, and so contagious that in the ten years between 1884 and 1894 no less than thirty thousand acres of vines were wiped out and the district plunged into financial ruin. Fortunately the Anaheim

[3] V. P. Carosso: *The California Wine Industry, 1830–1895* (University of California Press, 1951). This monograph has been drawn upon at numerous points in this chapter.

disease, after raging for a decade, began to lose its virulence and hence did not cause great losses in other areas. Its symptoms resemble those of the French vine disease *court noué*, which has been causing heavy losses since World War II in Mediterranean France. Its cause is evidently a virus infection.

There persisted also the problem of persuading the American people to become wine-drinkers. Arpad, son of Ágoston, put it well once when he said: "The great obstacle to our success . . . is, that the average American is a whisky drinking, water drinking, coffee drinking, tea drinking, and consequently a dyspepsia-inviting subject, who does not know the use or value of pure light wine taken at the proper time and in moderate quantities. The task before us lies in teaching our people how to drink wine, when to drink it and how much of it to drink." The task still wants accomplishment.

By 1909 production had grown to around 50,000,000 gallons. But something far harder to cope with than a bad reputation, or the phylloxera, or the Anaheim disease, lay in the offing. This was the threat of prohibition. Books have been written on the origin and diffusion of this disease, and its pathology; and I shall not go into that painful subject here, since it healed itself. The wine-makers treated it just as they had the phylloxera: first dismissing it as being of too little importance to bother about, then speaking of it with indignation, and finally growing panic-stricken. State after state was closed to the wine-makers. By 1915 they had their backs to the wall; and I know of no reading that is more affecting than the reports of the International Congress of Viticulture that was held concurrently with the

Panama-Pacific International Exposition of 1915. Since there was a war on, most of the wine-men who were to have been delegates either were fighting one another in the trenches or had already been killed. The rest were Americans, most of them old friends anyway; and the theme that ran through everything they had to say was the rising menace of prohibition, how to stop it, how to make people realize that wine is the friend of temperance and the innocent victim of the prejudice against spirits. Resolutions were passed denouncing prohibition as "virtual confiscation of property without payment," and plans for campaigns of "public education" were gloomily discussed. Yet most of the delegates knew, even then, that the days of their industry were numbered. The prohibitionists won their battle in due course. Thousands of acres of excellent vines were grubbed up and the laxative and familiar prune planted in their places. The Eighteenth Amendment was written into law, and the California growers and vintners found themselves with large stocks of mature and aging wine in their cellars, representing much labor and a very considerable investment. The deadline was January 16, 1920, and the official ruling was that all wine for export must be on board ship and actually out of port by that day.

Thus, after a short and exciting life of little more than sixty years, which is approximately the life span of a good sherry, California's wine-making industry was destroyed—or so most people thought. When prohibition became the law, California had some 700 wineries. Of these, 520 were in the coast counties—256 in Sonoma County, 120 in Napa, and the rest divided largely between Santa Clara, Contra Costa, Alameda, Mendocino, and Santa Cruz. In the interior valleys there were some 158 wineries; and in southern California there were 22, many of these being of large capacity. A few stuck it out, keeping body and soul together by the legal production of sacramental wine. Some held on for a year or two as bonded wineries and warehouses, then passed out of existence; many of them sold their equipment intact to the great bodegas of the province of Mendoza in Argentina. With the disappearance of these went many proud names—Gundlach-Bundschu, William Hoelscher, Lachman and Jacobi, A. Finke's Widow. . . .

Yet prohibition actually brought a new and unexpected prosperity to many growers of wine grapes. Its effect on the affairs of California's vineyardists was one of the most grotesque and ridiculous chapters in the whole farcical story. *Prohibition proved merely to be a ban on superior wines.* Congress had left a loophole which allowed the making of wines at home. So instead of selling their grapes to the wineries, many of the growers simply loaded them into refrigerator cars and shipped them east, especially to the big cities with large foreign-born populations. And here developed another surprise. The amateur wine-makers of the East knew nothing of the difference between one grape and another. It is notorious that the best wine grapes are not the most beautiful, so these amateurs walked right by them in the markets and leaped upon the prettiest. The small and unimpressive Cabernet, the undistinguished-looking Pinot, the thin-skinned and sticky Riesling and Sémillon —these went begging, while those with thick skins and placid dispositions and no capacity for producing superior wines were snapped up. The result was an almost complete reversal in the order of prices. The grapes that brought high prices were the common black varieties, chiefly the Alicante Bouschet, a beautiful grape which yields a coarse wine. The planting of this and the other mediocre but productive varieties was therefore greatly stimulated.

So the bulk vineyards flourished, and the growers who had labored for quality were forced to cut down their better plants and graft the cheap and highly productive varieties upon their roots. Under prohibition California's annual production of wine grapes doubled, and only the conscientious growers of fine vines were penalized.

But for three things, no fine vines at all would have survived the long night of prohibition. One is the outrageous and unreasonable love that some growers hold for their vineyards. Such growers will put up with a great deal. Another was of course the steady demand for sacramental wines. The third was the rise and growth of the concentrate industry, with the assistance of the Federal Government. The technique of concentrating grape juices by evaporation or by freezing had long been known. The growers banded together and called themselves Fruit Industries, Ltd. They obtained a loan of three million dollars from that same government which was engaged in enforcing prohibition. The idea was that this agency would sell concentrates to amateurs, who in turn could dilute them to the original consistency of the juice and allow them to ferment in their pantries. Then, thanks to the legal ingenuity of Mrs. Mabel Walker Willebrandt, a Portia of the time, a technique for "servicing" these concentrates was worked out. It became possible to place one's order with a salesman, who installed the dilute concentrate of whatever type might be desired, inoculated it with a culture of pure wine yeast, and pre-

sided over its fermentation, finally filtering, bottling, capping, and labeling the wine that was thus made. The rise of
this industry was an inspiring demonstration of the American spirit of "know-how" and "can-do," and it also brought
some relief to those stubborn fools who had refused to
sacrifice their good vines.

So the end of prohibition found California with its head
bloody but unbowed, ready and indeed eager to heal its
wounds and rebuild its partly shattered domain. How well
it has done this is a matter for another chapter.

CHAPTER V

American Wine Today

One fine day in 1933 the experiment which President
Hoover had described as "noble in motive and far-
reaching in purpose" was brought to a close. Repeal raised
the curtain on the tattered fragments of a once vigorous
and expanding agricultural industry. Wineries were physi-
cally run-down and financially feeble. Vineyards were full
of the wrong kinds of grapes. Worst of all, there was a
shortage of experienced wine-men. So the first post-repeal
years were chaotic. Both in California and in the East, there
existed limited quantities of sound wine—some made under
bond in anticipation of repeal, some made under the privi-
lege of making sacramental wine, and some that had survived the years of prohibition. But most of the wine of
those first post-repeal years was poor stuff. We need not
dwell on the gruesome details. Public ignorance provided a
period of grace in which the wine-men could pull themselves together.

American winegrowers made good use of the breathing-
space. What they did during the eight or nine years following repeal was in fact extraordinary. After the first flurry

54

of confusion, wine-making technique was brought up to date and, indeed, carried beyond customary practice in the older wine-making countries. Quality in the loftier sense remained limited by the small supply of really superior grapes, but in terms of soundness and stability American wines were soon beyond reproach. There was a good public response, too. In the year 1934 (the first full year of repeal) consumption of all wine in the United States [1] amounted to about 37,843,000 gallons, of which about 4,000,000 gallons were imported. By the year of our entry into World War II, 1941, consumption of tax-paid wine [2] had jumped to about 104,000,000 gallons, the fraction of imported wine remaining at about the same figure of 4,000,000 gallons. Prior to prohibition the largest total consumption in any one year in our country had been 54,000,000 gallons. Of the 1941 consumption of 104,000,000 gallons, 88,000,000 gallons were made in California. California has continued to hold this dominant position, though there are some interesting qualifications on the gross figure which will be mentioned presently.

The war created exceptional conditions for winegrowing. Imports were practically eliminated; and the conversion of whisky distilleries to war production of alcohol broadened the market for wines. These conditions led to the much discussed "invasion" of the liquor interests into winemaking. So the huge Roma winery (but not the vineyards!) became the property of Schenley, as did the name (old as California wine names go) of Cresta Blanca. So, in a parallel set of acquisitions, the huge Italian-Swiss properties went to

---

[1] Excluding an estimated 33,000,000 gallons of homemade wine.
[2] Again not including homemade wine of about the same amount.

National Distillers, along with others. These were the most spectacular but not the only weddings between wine-making capacity and whisky money. Naturally they caused apprehension, for the liquor business is in certain respects the antithesis of the wine trade. Yet the effects of the "invasion" were by no means wholly bad. The whisky people brought financial strength to an industry that was badly in need of it. They brought their skill in advertising and distribution. Nor did they swallow up the industry. Their main concern was with the mass production of "standard" wine and particularly of the cheap fortified sweet wines. The invasion touched none of the fine old Eastern producers of still and sparkling wines, nor more than a few of their counterparts in California. A spirit of give and take between the invaders and the independents has yielded a *modus vivendi* that is tolerable if it is entirely pleasing to no one.[3]

2: IN CALIFORNIA

California has something over 500,000 bearing acres yielding 3,000,000 tons of grapes a year more or less. But grape-growing is several things in California: table-grape-growing, raisin-growing, winegrowing. Thus roughly one half of the total grape crop ends up in the wineries for the production of 130,000,000 to 180,000,000 gallons of wine a year. A breakdown of this production for 1962 reveals the special and somewhat lopsided character of the industry at that time:

[3] In the past few years a new trend toward mergers in part involving whisky money has developed.

	GALLONS
Table wine	64,911,000
Dessert wine	96,436,000
Vermouth, apéritif wine	15,911,000
Sparkling wine	2,140,000
TOTAL	179,398,000

Thus the tail wagged the dog. Only about one third of the production was accounted for by still table wines. The rest were specialties, mainly fortified wines, which serve other ends than table wines and go mainly to a market interested in alcoholic kick at a low price. The California wine industry is really two industries, concerned with essentially different products, though, to be sure, there is much overlapping. Many table-wine producers make or at least market dessert wines in order to complete their commercial "line," and the big dessert-wine people are often makers or bottlers of some table wines as well, for the same reason.

But not long afterwards a curious thing happened. Year by year the production of table wines began to creep up on that of the fortified wines in response to a change of public demand. In 1966 it almost reached the halfway mark, and in 1967 for the first time this mark was passed. In that year, from the point of view of the amateur of table wine, the tail stopped wagging the dog. The table-wine inventory in 1970 accounted for 150,000,000 gallons out of a total inventory of 267,000,000 gallons, much more of it red than white. Let us see what each of the state's regions has to offer.

Central Valley. This is pre-eminently the region of cheap

dessert-wine production, which is concentrated in Fresno, Kern, Tulare, Madera, and San Joaquin counties. The cloudless summers, with their intense heat and negligible humidity, plus rich soil and irrigation, provide huge crops and high sugar content. Sugar and alcohol are the desiderata in the production of these wines, and the classical port and sherry grape varieties are scarcely known by name, let alone grown.[4] But most of California's "standard" table wine is also produced in the valley. By and large, the same grape varieties are used for both: Alicante Bouschet, Carignane, Zinfandel, Mataro, and Mission for the red; Thompson's Seedless and Tokay strippings for a far larger proportion of the white than anyone cares to admit. These standard wines are as a rule well made on a highly industrialized basis. They run rather high in alcohol (12½ to 13 per cent by volume). They are short on fruitiness, rather coarse in flavor, and deficient in acidity. They are stabilized as quickly as possible and moved promptly to market, a substantial proportion in bulk for local bottling elsewhere under private labels, or bottled at the winery in gallons. They are characteristic hot-country wines, and certainly superior in quality to the run of French *ordinaire*. The red is almost always better than the white—again, a characteristic of hot-country wines. There is currently a vogue for rosé wines and for inexpensive "mellow" red table wines having a slight sweetness. The vogue for rosé is sound, that for the other seems less promising for the long pull. A certain proportion of this wine is set aside to be blended with wines of superior quality (meaning, usually, better color, a fruitier

---

[4] The acreage of true port grapes in California is largely concentrated on a single property, the Ficklin vineyard near Madera.

aroma, less alcohol, and higher acidity) brought in from the north-coast counties. To assure supplies for blending, many of the big Central Valley firms have complementary north-coast properties, or working arrangements with the north-coast wineries. The resulting wines are the Burgundy, the Sauternes, the Claret, the Chablis, and lately the Rosé of the familiar nationally distributed brands.

Southern California. West and south of Los Angeles, mainly in San Bernardino, Los Angeles, and San Diego counties, is a region that is separated by mountains from the great Central Valley. Its climate is to some extent tempered by exposure to wind and moisture from the Pacific. Here also most of the production is in the hands of a few large producers; and here is the famous Guasti winery, which is now known as Brookside. But there are numerous small producers in addition, who dispose of their wines locally. Though the standard grape varieties of the Central Valley dominate here, too, they do not do so to quite the same extent. Here, for example, are considerable plantings of the Italian red-wine varieties such as Barbera, Freisa, and Grignolino. And though the wines of the large producers are blended to a standard, there is a good deal of diversity among the wines of the smaller producers. There is an engaging roughness about some of these wines which recalls the wines to be had, out of the barrel and into the pitcher, in the towns of Tuscany and Piedmont. Red-wine production far exceeds white, and properly.

Southern Coast Counties. This region is not well named, for it is neither coastal nor southern. It consists of the area bordering on the long southern wing of San Francisco Bay. Most of its vineyards and wineries are in two counties,

Alameda, lying east of the bay, and Santa Clara, lying at its southern end.

Alameda contains two distinct districts. One of them, the more famous, is the Livermore Valley, which lies just east of and parallel to the bay, being separated by a low range of mountains. This is a district long famous for its white wines, particularly those of the Sauternes types. The wine-grower names associated historically with the district are Concannon, Wente, and Cresta Blanca. Cresta Blanca is now merely a division of the huge Schenley organization, and a "label." Concannon and Wente continue as independents, winegrowers in the literal sense. The "château" types of these producers, naturally sweet and made of the classic blend of Sémillon, Sauvignon Blanc, and Muscadelle, are comparable to French Sauternes. The drier wines, produced from Sémillon and Sauvignon Blanc, legitimately recall good dry white Graves. And since repeal the Wentes have pioneered in the planting of Pinot Blanc and Chardonnay for the production of very good wines of the white Burgundy type. Other, less familiar winegrowing names are those of Ruby Hill and Loretto, producers who have occasionally received awards at the annual judging at the Sacramento State Fair. The red wines of the Livermore Valley, though above the run of California wines,[5] have never equaled the whites in quality and reputation, which is unusual under California conditions.

The second of the Alameda County districts is wholly different in character, lying closer to the bay, between Irvington and Mission San Jose. The outstanding producers here are Llords and Elwood and Weibel vineyards. The

[5] Because based on superior hot-climate grapes, such as Barbera and Mourastel.

area is not known for a specialty, as is the Livermore Valley. Plantings are mixed, but with a fairly good acreage of superior varieties both white and red. I recall a fine Los Amigos Zinfandel of several years ago, a wine that left no doubt as to the ability of this variety to produce good wine in the right circumstances, and a good (sweet) Black Muscat from Weibel. The Weibel sparkling wines are clean and well made, though they have the limitations imposed on all of the California champagnes by the un-champagne-like climate. Another producer of good wines in this district is David Bynum.

The broad and incredibly fertile Santa Clara Valley is in effect a southern extension of the depression partly filled by San Francisco Bay. It is protected from the Pacific by the Santa Cruz Mountains and separated from the great Central Valley by another range on its east. In spite of suburban encroachments it is still the land, par excellence, of the prune; and in this valley also lie most of the vineyards of the county that bears its name. Santa Clara County produces three times as much wine as Alameda. In general, the climate grows hotter and quality decreases with distance from the bay, so that much of the product of its southern sector resembles the "standard" wines of the Central Valley or goes into dessert wines. But a significant proportion of the Santa Clara Valley wines may be classed as superior. Many of the smaller growers habitually sell their crop to the large wineries, reserving only a portion of it to make into wine themselves; this they may sell in bulk or at retail. Others ferment, but sell their young wines regularly to the larger concerns for blending and finishing. Of the better-known names in the valley proper, Almadén Vineyard (the old Charles le Franc property) is a producer of an agreeable champagne and a full line of still red and white wines besides. Almadén has made ambitious plantings of superior varieties such as Cabernet, Pinot Noir, Chardonnay, Gewurz Traminer, and Riesling, and is intent on producing the best wines possible within the limitations of the climate. Its Grenache Rosé has had a pioneering success. Not all of the wines bottled under the Almadén label are of Almadén production. It is a beautifully managed property—indeed, one of the show places of the industry. A still bigger producer was B. Cribari & Sons,[6] at Madrone, specializing in popular-priced and bulk wines. The Mirassou vineyards have good plantings of superior grapes (much of the good Mirassou wine has gone to Paul Masson and Almadén). And on the western slope of the valley, in the outskirts of the charming town of Los Gatos, are the vineyards, winery, and home buildings of the Jesuit Novitiate of Los Gatos, which does an extensive business in sacramental wines, but produces some superior table and dessert wine as well. The Novitiate wines represent a successful compromise between quality (which is rarely associated with quantity) and mass production and distribution.

Santa Clara County embraces not only the fertile valley floor but a substantial segment of the Santa Cruz Mountains. Rising abruptly out of the town of Saratoga, one enters an area of great promise (still largely unexploited) for quality wine production in California. The pioneer in this mountain area was Paul Masson, the champagne-producer of pre-prohibition fame. After prohibition the name and

[6] Cribari is now just a label. This winery was sold by the Cribaris to the Lucky Lager (beer) people, who made a large investment in vineyards and plant but then abandoned the project.

the mountain vineyard were taken over by a quasi-legend-
ary young man, Martin Ray, who extended the plantings
of superior varieties and who proceeded to make a series of
exceptionally good (and expensive) table wines, of which
the Gamay stood out as a revelation of California's possibilities. The name of Paul Masson has now passed into the pos-
session of aggressive merchandisers who appear to be more
concerned with national distribution than with the climate
and soil of the Santa Cruz range. Martin Ray has found another mountaintop: his small output is top quality.

There are a number of other mountain winegrowers
within the borders of the county, but owing to a less scru-
pulous choice of varieties and less capable handling in the
cellar the wines are not outstanding. Still in the mountains
lie a number of other good vineyards. And to the south of
here in San Benito County near Hollister is a favored district which includes the former (and famous) Valliant
property plus huge new plantings of premium varieties by
Almadén. Over a range of hills to the west near Salinas is a
wholly new winegrowing district that is being pioneered
by Paul Masson, Wente, and Mirassou and shows great
promise.

This quick summary of the southern coast counties is
completed by reference to a number of vineyards along the
eastern arm of San Francisco Bay in Contra Costa County.
The influence of the bay favors certain superior varieties
that do not do at all well in the hotter parts of the region.
The Digardi vineyard, near Martinez, produces a Gamay
that has several times won recognition in competitions—a
wine which strengthens the belief that the Gamay, *not* the

63

Pinot Noir, offers the best hope for true Burgundy characteristics in California.

North-Coast Counties. The two counties of Napa and Sonoma, lying north of San Francisco Bay, plus the extension of the Sonoma Valley which lies in Mendocino County, produce more superior red and white table wine from more wineries than all the rest of the state together.

The town of Napa is easily and quickly reached from San Francisco by the Golden Gate Bridge. The town is not itself a winegrowing center, for here at the broad lower end of the valley the cooling effect of the bay breezes is still powerful, and vineyards are not numerous. It is a characteristic of both Napa and Sonoma valleys that their climate grows steadily hotter as one proceeds north and away from the bay. A few miles north of Napa, approaching Yountville, the valley narrows and its sides steepen. By the time Oakville is reached, there can no longer be any doubt of the main concern of this valley; and from then on, along both sides of the road, through Rutherford and St. Helena up to Calistoga, not only is there a dense concentration of vineyards but the highway itself displays a succession of wineries bearing familiar names. Beyond Calistoga the vineyards thin out again as one branch of the highway passes over into non-viticultural Lake County and the other branch swings west into the upper end of Sonoma.

Two or three points about Napa Valley (and Sonoma as well) ought to be made clear. One is that this is essentially red-wine, rather than white-wine, country. Some good white wines are made, to be sure, just as good white wines are made in the Italian Piedmont and Tuscany. But as in those celebrated regions, they are exceptions. Napa Valley produces twice as much red as white, and Sonoma Valley four times as much.

Another important point is that not all of the wines from these valleys are "fine" wines. Most of them are not. Here as everywhere else the heavy-producing ordinary varieties are preponderant. But the ordinary varieties produce wine of better quality here than they do in the other areas. Carignane wine from, say, Fresno, is coarse, crude, and earthy. Carignane wine from Napa Valley is well balanced and agreeable; and Carignane produces an even better rosé. A Zinfandel from Stockton or Lodi lacks color and is "hot" and flat-tasting. A Zinfandel from Napa or Sonoma is fruity and lively and sometimes very nearly "elegant" if well matured. The standard wines of this region are consistently superior to the standard wines of other regions, and are almost always the best buys in the popular-priced range.

A third point to remember is that some north-coast wineries are not at all averse to blending, as the occasion may demand, "stretching" the wines of their better grape varieties with cheaper and plentiful wines of their own or their neighbors. The whole industry, for that matter, does a great deal of trading stocks of wine. This can be frustrating to the would-be connoisseur who wants to track down a given wine to its point of origin. But it is in no sense a dishonorable practice provided no deception is involved, and indeed a blended wine may often be superior to any one of its constituents. The California Wine Association (formerly Fruit Industries, Ltd.) is a co-operative of producers in many parts of California which has built its business on the artful blending of the wines of its constituent members. There exist several houses of good reputation which are not producers at all but confine themselves to the purchase, blending, and cellar treatment of other people's wines.

These generalizations out of the way, it may be useful to make a quick tour of the district, beginning at the lower end of Napa Valley and working north on Route 29. Beg or borrow a California road map and the course of the tour will be much clearer.[7]

First come the Mont La Salle vineyards, mass producers of middle-quality wine marketed mainly under the Christian Brothers label. These are off to the west of the town of Napa and not visible from the road.

Beyond Yountville and approaching Oakville, the vineyards begin to thicken; and at Rutherford, on the left, is the superb Inglenook vineyard, now a part of the Allied-Heublein merger and hence being watched for signs of change. Vines begin at the highway and extend back to the forested hills. The picturesque stone cellars stand well back from the road, entirely surrounded by vines. Inglenook is one of the best of all the California producers and is especially admired for its Cabernet and its highly individual and rather light-colored Pinot Noir. It has plantings of other superior red-wine varieties, such as Gamay and the Italian grape Charbono. The Charbono yields a sturdy wine much resembling superior French Côtes du Rhône. Like the latter, it really ought to have ten years in bottle—something the economics of California wine production forbid. Inglenook's white wines display both the strengths and the weaknesses of California white wines generally, being more in-

[7] Normal changes of ownership, plus the onrush of suburbia, will be found to have altered some of the details of what follows.

teresting for their body and softness than for their fruitiness. The most characteristic of these is possibly the White Pinot, which is made not from the true Pinot but from the Chenin, or Pinot de la Loire.

Adjacent to the Inglenook plantings lies the still more impressive Beaulieu vineyard, with its handsome house and elaborately landscaped grounds. The winery itself, a plain square building that is equipped to protect the bins of bottled wines against earthquake shock, lies across the road on the east side. In the matter of consistent quality, recognition, and prizes, Inglenook and Beaulieu are practically on a par. It is always a toss-up, for example, which of these will produce the better Cabernet in a given year. It is generally agreed that the Beaulieu Cabernet of 1936 is the best California red wine since repeal, but Inglenook has made Cabernets the equal of a fine French Saint-Émilion. The Beaulieu Pinot Noir is entirely different in character from that of Inglenook, despite the fact that the two are grown side by side. The second-string Beaulieu wines are a bit of a drop from their prize-winners.

Between Rutherford and St. Helena the procession of vineyards and wineries is more or less continuous. Most conspicuous of the latter is the unglamorous but well-equipped winery of Louis M. Martini, another of those which manage to combine large-scale production and distribution with premium quality. The Martinis, father and son, are devoted and ceaseless experimenters in the vineyards and in wine-making techniques. The wines are consistent award-winners in competitions (though they seem to win more silver medals than gold), and are based on important plantings of the superior varieties.

Just beyond the town of St. Helena, on the left, is the

67

picturesque old Beringer winery, and beyond that the once-famous Greystone winery, now simply a Christian Brothers storage cellar and show place. A bit farther along, down a lane on the right side, is the old Charles Krug winery. This has for some time been the property of the Mondavi family. Both winery and vineyards have been much expanded and improved. Plantings of the best "varietals" are being increased year by year. The Mondavis are concentrating on superior white wines, such as Traminer, Riesling, and Pinot Blanc, and are seeking to overcome the characteristic heaviness of most California white wine by close attention to such matters as early picking, low-temperature fermentation, and early bottling. Robert Mondavi has recently branched off and established a separate winery.

From here on, the vineyards begin to thin out again, though some of the wines of Freemark Abbey, Schramsberg, Hans Kornell, and Heitz demonstrate that the potential for high quality has by no means thinned out. The potential output of superior red and white wines from the upper Napa Valley is limited only by the market and by the number of those who are willing to plant the best varieties and make the effort.

Before passing over the divide from Napa Valley into the head of Sonoma Valley, a word ought to be said for another and much less conspicuous group: those winegrowers whose concern is quality in small quantity, such as J. Leland Stewart, whose Souverain vineyard and winery hang on the eastern lip of the valley above St. Helena; the J. F. M. Taylors, who literally scooped off the top of one of the Mayacamas mountains to plant for themselves a vineyard of upland Pinot Chardonnay and Pinot Blanc; and Frederick McCrea, with plantings of fine white varieties. These, and a few others like them,[8] are obsessed with the challenge of quality, and yet, precisely because they do not produce on a large scale, must contend with great difficulties in the matter of distribution and its costs. Practically speaking, they must content themselves with the California market—at any rate, until they can find some means of banding together for mass shipments elsewhere.

Sonoma and Napa valleys are parallel, Sonoma lying closer to the Pacific, and they are separated by the Mayacamas range. But Sonoma has twice the length, and in fact has twice as many wineries and produces nearly twice as much wine. In terms of quality, each of the valleys has its partisans among California's connoisseurs. A fair statement would be that Napa produces more really notable individual vintages, but that enough are produced in Sonoma to wreck the argument for Napa's *intrinsic* superiority. A would-be moderator might insist that the best sites of all are those (largely unexploited) which lie well up in the mountains between the two.

To make the tour of Sonoma Valley from north to south (the route through Napa Valley was from south to north), it is necessary to begin in Mendocino County, around the town of Ukiah. Here the wine made is nine tenths red, and there are some good plantings of Barbera, Petite Sirah, and other medium-to-fine varieties. No one winery stands out conspicuously for a fine specialty, though that of Parducci & Son, running counter to the local preference for red-wine

[8] The number has been increasing lately.

69

production, has won medals for a dry white wine of the French Colombard grape.

South of Ukiah there is a long stretch of valley in which the vine takes second place to other crops, including hops. Then, at the very border of Sonoma County, the vines begin again, to continue in an unbroken succession for a good thirty miles or more. Vineyard names long associated with the area are those of Walter Sink, E. Berti, and Hollis M. Black. But in general the vineyards are anonymous because this region around Cloverdale and indeed the whole of the upper valley are dominated, in scale of operations, by the Italian Swiss Colony, which began in the mid nineteenth century as a sort of utopian winegrowing colony but since repeal has been the football of promoters and financial interests. A visit to Italian Swiss Colony today is like a visit to the great wine-factories of the Central Valley. One beholds with awe the outdoor cistern of concrete, with flower beds on top, which is used for making the massive blends. One threads one's way along overhead balconies in the storage rooms, passes from one building to another by covered bridges over railway sidings, pauses to observe a huge snow-covered filter through which torrents of chilled wine are being passed toward the automatic fillers and capping machines. Italian Swiss, originator of the famous "Tipo," [9] now finds this trade-mark being applied to such novelties as chianti-like flasks full of port or muscatel; and the list of wine types and brand names now issuing from this huge winery is legion: "varietals" of superior quality under the "Asti" label, sound standard wines under the "Gold Medal" label, and trainloads of bulk wine

[9] That is, Tipo Chianti, meaning chianti type.

for Eastern bottlers under no name at all. Italian Swiss is a subsidiary now of Allied Grape Growers, which in turn belongs to Heublein—basically a high-pressure marketer.

South of Italian Swiss (which enjoys the post-office address of Asti) is to be found a row of wineries on the west side of the highway bearing names like Seghesio, Mazzoni, Pastori, and Pedroncelli and producing wines that are indeed the counterparts of the good wines of the Italian Piedmont, Emilia, and Tuscany, not "fine" perhaps, but not so bad either. How much "fine" wine is produced, after all, in Italy? And so it continues through Geyserville and down the road to Healdsburg: Nervo, Frei Brothers, Emilia Oneto, and so on. But listing the names of producers along here is a treacherous business because of turnover: a listing is obsolete by the time it is printed.

As one passes south of Healdsburg, the Italianate procession continues. Then as Santa Rosa is approached, the valley widens and there are tributaries from the west, so that the wineries cease to line the borders of the highway. Farthest west near Guerneville in the Russian River Valley is the champagne vineyard of F. Korbel & Bros., now property of the Heck family. The Hecks have expanded the operation and produce still wines also. About halfway between Guerneville and Santa Rosa are the former vineyards and winery of Valliant and Sons, bought by Hiram Walker during the wartime "invasion" of the whisky interests but later disposed of to Elmo Martini and Enrico Prati, members of families rooted in Sonoma Valley winegrowing. Martini & Prati ranks second in size to Italian Swiss.

Just north of Santa Rosa (and getting back to the main highway) is the site of the old Fountaingrove vineyard, possessor of a romantic and checkered history and (once)

7 I

of some of the best blocks of red-wine grapes in California. Following repeal it produced some famous red wines, especially Cabernets; but it was plagued by problems and now has given way to suburbia. The Fountaingrove brand name is owned by Martini & Prati.

Below Santa Rosa the highway branches, the main road heading due south for San Francisco. On the other road, Route 12, the sequence of vineyards and wineries thins out for a while. But then, approaching the town of Sonoma, there is a cluster of several producers of real note. Most distinguished of these is Hanzell Vineyards, the luxurious plaything of the late J. D. Zellerbach, whose object was to produce a Pinot Chardonnay and a Pinot Noir equal to the best produced on the French Côte d'Or. With his death it passed to Mr. and Mrs. Douglas Day, whose hope it was to keep property and ideal intact.

Not far is the Buena Vista vineyard. Vineyard and winery are the old Ágoston Haraszthy property, the pioneer winery of northern California, bought and restored by Mr. and Mrs. Frank Bartholomew and only recently resold to a worthy successor. The property is a state historical monument. A bit farther is the Sebastiani winery, producer of good, sound, middle-grade wines and some superior ones.

Beyond the town of Sonoma on the road back to the city of Napa where this tour began, there is one final outburst. This consists of extensive plantings by Beaulieu, Louis M. Martini, and several others of the finest cool-country winegrape varieties such as Pinot Chardonnay and Pinot Noir—the object being to take advantage of the cool breezes blowing in from San Pablo Bay, an arm of the San Francisco Bay. Planting in this area is still going on. Then the road merges with the highway from Napa to San Francisco. The great-

circle tour has been completed, a sketchy one and in
some respects perhaps an unjust one. Not all the producers
of good wines could possibly be mentioned, and there seems
no point in mentioning the producers of bad. But the plain
truth is that viticultural California has not yet reached the
point where a guide comparable, say, to the good guides to
the French winegrowing districts can possibly be written.
The pattern is not sufficiently stable: the winegrowers,
even the best of them, are not yet sufficiently certain what
goals they strive for. And yet the very fluidity of the winegrowing scene gives it a special fascination. The amateur of
fine French Burgundies must often have wished that he
might have tasted Burgundies during the days before men
knew that the Clos of Vougeot and of Tart were better
than their neighbors—during the days, in short, when the
finding of the best Burgundies was still an adventure and
there were no charts and guides to point the way. Such is
still to a large extent the state of affairs in California's north-
coast counties—and will be for many years. Some few
wines are regularly crowned, but they have many rivals
both present and potential.

3: ELSEWHERE

Still, California does possess defined viticultural regions, the
limitations and possibilities of which are fairly well known.
The situation in the rest of the United States (what we may
call the non-vinifera United States) is entirely different.

To begin with, there is no such volume of production
and density of vineyards as in California. Year in and year
out, California produces eighty-five to ninety per cent of all

wine produced commercially in the United States. Against California's annual production of 190,000,000, more or less, the rest of the United States produces in the neighborhood of 30,000,000 gallons.

A second point is that much of this non-California wine is really something else. Such are the "wines" derived from fruits other than the grape—the blackberry and loganberry wines, the peach, apple, strawberry, and citrus wines. These are essentially cordials, heavily fortified with sugar and alcohol and agreeable enough when sipped with cookies, but sold chiefly, alas, as cheap intoxicants. The production of these is thinly scattered over many parts of the United States. In the same category must be placed much of the wine produced from highly flavored grape varieties like the Concord in the Northeast and Middle West and the Scuppernong and other rotundifolias of the Southern states. Such also are the kosher wines that have had so substantial a commercial success during the last few years. These are wines with a base of labrusca, usually Concord, grapes which are fermented with a large excess of sugar but do not have a particularly high alcoholic content. They are more properly classed as confectionery than as wine.

Third, much of what passes statistically as non-California wine actually originates in California. This is explained by the fact that a great many Eastern wineries customarily produce blended wines. Wines from Eastern grapes may be "stretched" by the addition of California grape concentrate, or by the addition of cheap, neutral wine brought in from California by tank car. There exist also some Eastern producers of domestic "champagne" who never see a grape: what they do is buy California still wine in bulk and bring

74

it east for processing. These practices are legitimate, and some of the resulting wines are of tolerable quality. Yet all of them go down in the statistics as "Eastern" wine and so help to build up a false picture. The entire production of truly non-California table wines, both still and sparkling, cannot amount, in all, to more than a few million gallons a year. This non-California production is rather specialized. A high proportion of it, amounting perhaps to one half of the total, is sparkling wine.[1] This is explained by the fact that a considerable acidity plus moderate alcoholic content plus lightness of body plus fruitiness are particularly desirable in making sparkling wines—and these are the normal characteristics of wines from the better Eastern-grown grapes.

Fourth, it is undeniable that Eastern producers have in the past been handicapped by their climate. Yields per acre run lower than in California, and production costs are higher. Use of the classic vinifera grapes has been impractical, and winegrowers have thus been compelled to rely on our American varieties with their relatively pronounced and special flavors. These have their ardent admirers, but they are specialties that do not appeal particularly to those whose taste in wine follows European models. This has been a heavy handicap, but it is now being reduced, slowly, with the help of the new "French hybrids." These vines now make it possible for the first time, outside of California, to produce wines lacking the "foxiness" and other pronounced flavors that we associate with American grapes.

With these generalizations in mind, we may proceed to

[1] New York State produced 4,592,437 gallons of sparkling wine in 1968, as against only 7,110,634 gallons produced in California.

a brief survey of American winegrowing outside of California.

New York. Outside of California, New York State is the largest producer. The vineyards are concentrated in four areas: the Hudson River Valley, the Finger Lakes region of central New York, the Chautauqua district, and the Niagara district.

The Hudson Valley district had a certain importance prior to prohibition, but has declined since, almost the only producer of consequence being the picturesque Bolognesi winery, near Highland. Here vineyards and winery occupy a spectacular site on a high bluff overlooking the river; the wines are conscientiously made, with pronounced "Eastern" characteristics of aroma and flavor. There are signs now of a new expansion of winegrowing in this district, and at least one substantial block of the French hybrids has been planted on the old High Tor property farther downstream. The proximity of this district to the big New York wine market is an obvious commercial advantage.

The Chautauqua district stretches westward from Buffalo along the southern shore of Lake Erie in New York (and in the northwest corner of Pennsylvania). The Concord dominates, but there are large and growing plantings of the French hybrids, and even a few of the hardier vinifera; and several wineries are now in production.

The Niagara district occupies the strip of land between Lake Erie and Lake Ontario, which is cut by the Niagara River. Lying between two large bodies of water, its climate is especially favorable to fruit-growing. On the Canadian side of the river there is an immense production of grapes for wine-making, consisting mainly of Concord, Catawba,

Niagara, and Delaware, with smaller plantings of Agawam and other old American sorts. During the past six or eight years there has been a trend toward the new French hybrids, the pioneer having been A. de Chaunac, the technical director of Bright's Wines, Ltd. The new vineyards have already produced small vintages of red and white wines of quite astonishing quality. The varieties that so far seem best adapted are Seibel 10878, Foch and Seibel 1000 for red wine and Seibel 10868, Seibel 5409, and Seibel 9110 for white, though much experimenting remains to be done. Winegrowing is less extensive on the American side of the river, but one substantial winery is in production, making both still and sparkling wines, and here too the tonnage of the good French hybrids is increasing rapidly.

However, New York really owes its reputation as a wine-producing state to the vintages that have been gathered for the better part of a century from vineyards lying along the Finger Lakes. These lakes, which lie in a cluster in the west-central part of the state, are long and narrow and very deep, with steeply rising sides. Their beauty is famous and their geology fascinating. For our purposes it is sufficient to say that their configuration causes local conditions peculiarly favorable to grape-growing. The largest of these lakes are Seneca and Cayuga, but grape-growing and wine-making are especially associated with Canandaigua and Keuka. The village of Hammondsport at the southern end of the latter is the center of the district, and most of the well-known New York State "champagnes" are produced near by. The two senior establishments are Great Western Producers (Great Western brand) and the

Gold Seal Vineyards (Gold Seal and Charles Fournier brands). Both are old firms whose names have long been associated with quality. The wines are bottle-fermented, and they derive their special characteristics from the careful handling and blending of wines of the Catawba, the Delaware, the Elvira, and small quantities of other varieties. They likewise produce a "line" of other wines, both table and dessert. These two firms, which once dominated the market, have long since made way for a third, Taylor Wine Company,[2] which actually controls more vineyard acreage than either of them. Taylor likewise produces a good sparkling wine of the same general characteristics, but a much larger proportion of its production consists of still wines. These three leaders all have considerable plantings of the new hybrids (Taylor perhaps the largest acreage and Gold Seal the biggest experimental collection) and are expanding them as rapidly as conditions permit. Gold Seal is also seeking once again to acclimatize the *viniferas*. Over a steep divide to the west of Keuka Lake lies Canandaigua Lake, with the village of Naples at its foot. Here are the Widmer Wine Cellars, fourth of the large Finger Lakes producers. The Widmers have always specialized in still wines and are well known for Eastern "varietals"—the light, unblended table wines of such varieties as Delaware, Catawba, Elvira, Diamond, and Vergennes—and sherry. The Widmers are first-rate technicians and meticulous grape-growers; they control a very large acreage and enjoy a high reputation in the trade.

There exist other wine-producers in the Finger Lakes district, but these four stand out in terms of both volume of production and quality.

[2] Ownership of Great Western recently passed to Taylor.

Other Areas. West of Cleveland, and centering on the port of Sandusky, there is a considerable winegrowing district, which is a sort of westward extension of the Chautauqua district. The vineyards are not only on the mainland, but on the islands a few miles offshore; and the grapes most used are Catawbas, known locally as "Cats." The most widely distributed of these wines, since repeal, have been those of Meier's Wine Cellars (which has island vineyards, and has a winery at Silverton, near Cincinnati, as well as at Sandusky). There are numerous other small wineries scattered among the lake-shore vineyards, most of which cater to a local trade. The best of these northern Ohio wines are probably the white sparkling wines, in which the characteristics of the Catawba are shown to good advantage. There is also a burst of new planting in the Ohio River Valley and in the central part of the state, mainly of French hybrids; and three small new wineries concentrating on dry table wines of good quality have recently been established.

Continuing west into Michigan, one finds another winegrowing district in the neighborhood of Paw Paw. Michigan wine-makers enjoy a substantial tax advantage, and as so often happens the relative immunity from competition has weakened the incentive to strive for quality. The Concord is the dominating grape; and the Concord, in the hands of the chemist, does duty for red wines, white wines, dessert wines, even "champagne." Little if any Michigan wine is exported to other states.

In the mid nineteenth century, Missouri wines, chiefly from vineyards along the banks of the Missouri River around Hermann, enjoyed an excellent reputation; and the American Wine Company, producing the sparkling wine known as Cook's Imperial, carried the name of Missouri far and wide. The American Wine Company is now a branch of Schenley, depending on California for the bulk of its raw material; and the winegrowing colony around Hermann, a victim of prohibition, is now being revived. In Arkansas and Oklahoma there are many small wineries. They are now turning to the French hybrids.

What has been said of Missouri is true likewise of the winegrowing industry around Charlottesville, Virginia. Once upon a time its red and white table wines from Catawba, Delaware, Norton, and Ives enjoyed a certain popularity. They are no more. Following repeal, an ambitious scheme for reviving Virginia winegrowing on a co-operative basis was projected; it has remained a dream.

And then there is the Northwest, meaning the states of Washington and Oregon. In each there is a sprinkling of small wineries, and has been for some time; those in the rainy coastal parts based on the old Eastern varieties and those in the dry interior valleys based on the vinifera. The interior valleys, meaning especially the Yakima Valley, have an immense potential, once the correct grapes are determined. These will inevitably be some of the hardiest north and central European vinifera, plus some of the better French hybrids. The state experiment station at Prosser has a fine experimental program underway, and a strong commercial initiative has lately been taken by the Seneca Foods Corporation, a big producer of grape and other fruit products, which has also entered wine production in the East. Look for some interesting results.

For the rest, what can be said? Alas, very little that is likely to interest the drinker of table wines. And yet, for the person in a position to detect it, there is much widely scattered but encouraging evidence of things to come—evidence that is almost everywhere associated with those remarkable new grape varieties, the French hybrids. For these grapes are spreading. The fact that the better-established wineries are turning to them has already been mentioned. Still more important for the future, perhaps, is the expanding use of them by small growers, by amateurs, by people who like wine and have found that a modest vineyard of these vines—a few dozen, perhaps, or a quarter-acre—amply takes care of their needs while providing recreation and exercise as well. There exists hardly a state where one or another of these varieties is not being grown. And each such cell of experiment tends to multiply. Neighbor learns from neighbor. The state experiment station comes to life and spreads the word. The agricultural press wakes up.

Nor do the amateurs always remain amateurs. A man finds a ready market for his surplus; soon he is expanding his planting to provide wine grapes for those who lack land for a vineyard of their own. Plans are afoot in a dozen states to make a gradual transition from amateur winegrowing to commercial winegrowing. Already in a number of cases that transition has been made, and good wines from the new hybrids begin to appear locally and to be known. But where vineyards are concerned, the pace is necessarily slow. It will be a long time before the pattern of winegrowing outside California has changed sufficiently to upset the statistics. It is changing nevertheless, and the people who are changing it are an odd and fascinating company. They are changing it by the enjoyable process of making good wine themselves from grapes they themselves grow.

CHAPTER VI

Wine-Making: the Principles

Wine-making, stripped down to its essentials, is simple and easy. Grapes are crushed into a clean, open receptacle, skins and all. Put in a moderately warm place, covered, and let alone, they will presently begin to ferment. The fermentation, which is indicated by a good deal of heaving and gurgling, continues for several days. When this begins to abate, the turgid new wine is pressed free of the solid matter, placed in another container, and lightly stoppered. This new wine continues to ferment, but much more gently, sometimes for a few days and sometimes for several months. At the end of that time the clear wine is separated from the sediment, and may be drunk, or bottled for keeping. Given clean receptacles, suitable grapes, and the assistance of a benign providence, one may thus procure drinkable wine. The boiling of an egg is hardly simpler.

The practical art of wine-making is only an elaboration of this primitive method. The chemist seeks to explain the natural process and to remove the uncertainty from it; the technician seeks to reduce the labor. The difference between primitive wine-making and enlightened wine-making is that one is laborious and uncertain in its result, the other less laborious and more certain. That is all.

And yet it will not do to overemphasize the simplicity of wine-making. That would be misleading. If a man comes down with a bad cold, his doctor gives him aspirin and tells him to go to bed. If he takes his aspirin and stays in bed, lo, he is well in a few days. But that is not to say that the process by which the body throws off infection and heals itself is simple. It is in fact a wonderfully complicated biological drama. The process by which grape juice becomes wine is no less complicated. We say that the juice "ferments." What do we mean? The biochemist would hesitate to give a flat answer. The more he learns, the more he realizes that there is still much to learn. And yet he is not entirely ignorant. The purpose of this chapter is to sketch out in fairly rudimentary terms what is known of the wine-making process, so that the practical wine-maker before proceeding to explicit instructions will have some insight into what he it doing.

2: ANATOMY OF THE WINE GRAPE

The differences between one wine and another have their beginning in the grapes. Each species and variety has qualities of its own which impart a special character to the wine. But all have elements in common. The three essential parts of the grape are the *seeds*, the *skin*, and the *pulp*. The *stems* also play a part in the making of some red wines. Roughly speaking, a bunch of grapes consists of the following:

	PERCENTAGE BY WEIGHT
Stems	3.83
Seeds	3.15
Skins	7.62
Pulp	85.40
	100.00

The *seeds* play a purely negative role in wine-making. That is, the wine-maker prefers not to crush any of them while crushing his grapes, for they contain an oil that does the wine no good.

The *skins* of grapes contribute a great deal to wine, chiefly coloring matter, aromatic substances, and tannin.

The coloring matter is not a single substance, but a complex of organic compounds still imperfectly understood. It is only slightly soluble in the fresh juice at moderate temperatures, but is dissolved by the alcohol developed during fermentation.[1] For this reason, in making red wines the juice is usually fermented in contact with the skins.

The aromatic substances located in the skins are even more complex chemically than the pigments and vary greatly according to grape variety. In most vinifera wine grapes the aroma is slight; but in some, particularly Cabernet, Riesling, Traminer, and the Muscat varieties, it is pronounced. Most of the American species, not to mention the standard American varieties, have aromatic substances to an overgenerous degree.

[1] The pigment may also be dissolved in the fresh juice by heating to 120° F. That is the way commercial grape juice gets its color.

84

The skins contribute a great deal of *tannin* to the wine. This is the source of the agreeable astringency, or puckery taste, in such wines as Chianti and most red Bordeaux. Tannin also has the valuable property of coagulating certain albuminous substances that occur naturally in grape juice and wine. By themselves, these substances would remain in suspension in the wine and prevent it from clearing. The coagulating process induced by the tannin helps to settle them out. A wine that contains adequate tannin becomes clear and bright with relative ease and stabilizes rapidly. The skin of the ripe grape also carries a thin waxy film called the bloom. This traps and holds the yeast spores as grapes ripen. Without yeasts there could be no fermentation. The bloom can trap other things that do wine no good, such as undesirable "wild" yeasts, harmful bacteria, molds, dust, and insecticides.

Pulp. In some varieties the pulp is crisp and compact; in most wine varieties it is soft and juicy. The juice from the squeezed pulp of "average" ripe grapes consists, approximately, of the following:

	PER-CENTAGE
Water	77.00
Fermentable sugar	20.00
Free acids (tartaric and malic chiefly)	.60
Potassium bitartrate (cream of tartar)	.63
Mineral salts (sulphates, phosphates, etc.), fats, nitrogenous compounds, pectic materials, and traces of other substances	1.77
	100.00

85

This is only an approximation. The proportions vary within wide limits. Thus water may vary from 55 to 85 per cent, and fermentable sugars from 12 to 30 per cent or even higher. Together, water and sugar comprise most of the juice, somewhere around 97 per cent. But the importance of the remaining constituents is greater than one might suppose from the quantities present. Notice that tannin is absent from the table, being in the skins and not in the juice.

The sugar content is of first interest to the wine-maker because the sugar in the must, or juice, is the source of the wine's alcohol. The sugars are principally dextrose and levulose. During fermentation the sugar is converted into almost equal quantities of carbon-dioxide gas (CO_2) and alcohol (C_2H_5OH). Thus fresh grape juice containing 20 per cent sugar produces a wine having about 10 per cent of alcohol. If you know the sugar content, you can estimate in advance the alcoholic content of the finished wine. The first rule of wine-making is this: *two degrees of sugar in the juice give one degree of alcohol in the wine.* Remember that and you are well on the road to becoming a wine-maker.

But experience has shown that yeasts will not usually continue their work of fermentation in an alcoholic solution of more than 14 or 15 per cent, even though there is still plenty of sugar to work on. Thus a must containing more than 28 per cent of sugar (remember the two-to-one rule) will rarely ferment out completely. An unwanted [2] residue of sweetness remains. On the other hand, experience has shown that a finished wine containing less than 8 per cent of alcohol is not only a thin and unpalatable bev-

[2] Unless, of course, one's object is to make sweet wine.

erage but a sickly and unstable one. In short, grapes that are deficient in sugar and grapes that have an excess of sugar are both unsatisfactory for dry, natural wines. Best results are to be had when sugar content is between 20 and 24 per cent. Remember this.

Sugar and water, then, account for 97 per cent or more of the fresh grape juice. The greater part of what is left consists of two organic acids, tartaric and malic, and their salts. Malic acid is found in many fruits—for example, apples and pears. Tartaric acid is conspicuously the acid of the grape. The two provide the "tartness" of the grapes, and the practical wine-maker lumps them together as "total acids" or "total acidity." Some varieties show high total acids and others low. Cool climates make for high total acids, and hot climates for low. In the heat and dryness of California low total acids are the rule. In northern European grape-growing districts and in the eastern part of the United States, total acids are usually high. The proportions between tartaric and malic acid are in most cases a function of the grape's ripeness. In unripe grapes the proportion of malic will be high. With increasing ripeness, the malic progressively disappears while the amount of tartaric present remains fairly stable, so that *relatively* the proportion of malic drops off sharply and the tartaric predominates.

Stems. The grape stems are frequently crushed into the fermenting-vat along with the grapes. If they are dry and woody, they contribute little to wine except tannin. If they are soft and pulpy, they may sometimes impart a certain bitterness to the wine. In contemporary commercial practice stems are usually removed mechanically at the time of crushing.

So we conclude the catalogue of substances that comprise the "average." Actually, the composition of two batches of grapes is never quite identical. The composition of any given grape varies steadily as it ripens on the vine. It varies as regards the numerous minor constituents that the wine-maker can do nothing about. It varies also in the two characteristics with which he is primarily concerned and which he can do something about, the *total sugar content* and the *total acidity*. As ripening proceeds, the proportion of sugar increases and that of the acid decreases. At a given moment the fruit reaches an optimum balance between sugar content and total acidity and is ripe from the wine-maker's point of view. The optimum point varies somewhat from one variety to another, but in general one may say that it is reached when sugar content has attained 20 to 23 per cent and total acidity has fallen not lower than 7 grams per liter.[3] The California wine-maker is concerned to pick his grapes before sugar is too high and acidity has fallen too low. In the East, on the other hand, where grapes rarely reach the maximum sugar content of which they are capable, the wine-maker seldom has to worry about insufficient acidity and is above all concerned to see that sugar content is adequate.

3: THE VINTAGE

In a simpler day the wine-maker judged entirely by taste and appearance in deciding when it was time to pick the grapes. But the sweetness of grapes can be deceptive. Acidity may

[3] Total acidity is usually indicated in grams per liter calculated as tartaric. See p. 127.

mask the presence of sugar, or a low-acid grape variety may seem much sweeter than it really is. It used to be, in the winegrowing countries, that the day for beginning the vintage was set by a village or district committee of experts; and it was an offense to gather the grapes before that day, since wine made from grapes not fully ripe might injure the reputation of an entire district. Nowadays the meticulous wine-maker may judge when to pick with the help of a simple instrument called a saccharometer. Even so, the decision when to pick remains one of the most difficult the winegrower must make, especially where the grapes ripen slowly and with difficulty. It is always tempting to pick when the fruit has reached a tolerable degree of ripeness and the crop is intact; further delay, though it may improve quality, may also bring disaster in the form of frost, persistent rains, or a swift invasion of ripe rot. The vintage may begin as early as mid-July in hot climates and as late as mid-November in Alsace and Germany.

In California the vintage is called "the crush." Whatever it is called, the essentials are the same the world over. The fruit is picked with small shears or hook-bladed knives; the pickers' baskets are emptied into larger containers; and thus to the winery. Careful wine-makers transport carefully; careless, carelessly.

The crush itself is variously organized. The classic pattern is that of the winegrower properly speaking—the proprietor who grows his own grapes and carries right on through to the finished wine. But there are many other patterns. In the great mass-production areas the functions of grower and "converter" are divided, usually to the detriment of the quality. The farmer picks his crop and sells it to a large central winery, at which point his interest is ended; and the wine that the "converter" produces is no better than the grapes he buys. Or the farmer pools his interest with others to form a co-operative. There are huge grower-winery co-operatives in California, as there are in southern France. Wine from co-operatives is rarely the best, and rarely the worst. Whatever the prevailing pattern of custom, the first step in wine-making is the crushing of the fruit. Here and there in backward areas the crushing is still done by foot, but crushers operated by hand or power are easier. From the crusher the must is pumped, or falls or is heaved, into the fermenting-vat.

4: THE YEASTS

It is not until the must is in the vats that the yeasts get down to work. Although much has been learned of the nature of fermentation since the time of Pasteur, there still remain many steps in the process of alcoholic fermentation which no man understands. It was not until 1857, when Pasteur initiated his great series of researches leading to the discovery and isolation of the living organisms called wine yeasts, and definitely linked their vital processes with fermentation, that it was really understood at all. He demonstrated that in wine-making the fermentation always proceeds in the presence of living yeasts. He embodied his conclusion in the famous observation that: "the chemical act of fermentation is essentially a phenomenon correlative with a vital act, commencing and ceasing with the latter. I am of the opinion that alcoholic fermentation never occurs without simultaneous organization, development, and multiplication of cells, or the continued life of cells already formed. *. . . If I am asked in what consists the chemical act whereby the sugar is decomposed and what is its real cause, I reply that I am completely ignorant of it.*"

Pasteur's discoveries represented a clean break with the assumptions then prevailing. This is well shown by a monograph on wine-making which was printed in the annual report of the U.S. Commissioner of Patents in the same year as Pasteur's first great discovery, 1857. Nowhere in the essay is it suggested that "organisms" are involved in the process; the word *yeast* is not used. Pasteur's discoveries were the real beginning of knowledge of the process of fermentation.

From Pasteur's time on, the secret of the process of alcoholic fermentation has slowly yielded to study. Pasteur concentrated attention upon the organisms present in all fermenting liquids. Buchner in 1897 carried knowledge a step forward by showing that fermentation is caused, not by the yeast itself, but by a substance that the yeast secretes. What Buchner did was to prepare a liquid from yeast, by crushing and filtering the cells, which was entirely free of all traces of living cellular matter. This liquid, to his astonishment, caused fermentation in a sugar solution even though no active yeast cells were present. What he did was to show that the active agent in fermentation is a *secretion* of the yeast cell and not the yeast itself. Buchner called the substance *zymase*. We now know that zymase is but one of numerous *enzymes*, substances of extreme complexity which are secreted by molds and bacteria and which are the effective agents, or catalysts, of numerous reactions that oc-

cur in nature. We know that the enzymes do not themselves enter into combination with the material of the reaction but in some mysterious manner achieve their effect
merely by contact, and that there is an enormous dispropor-
tion between their own small mass and the drastic changes
they are responsible for.

Stated in its simplest terms, then, alcoholic fermentation
consists of the breaking-down of sugar into alcohol and
carbon dioxide in the presence of zymase:

$$C_6H_{12}O_6 \text{ (zymase)} \xrightarrow{} 2\ C_2H_5OH + 2\ CO_2 + \text{(calories)}$$

(sugar)$$(alcohol)(carbon dioxide)

Buchner's discovery opened the way to other discoveries.
Summed up, they are: first, that the zymase which Buchner found is not one single activating substance, but a large
and still only partially understood complex of substances,
each of which has its part to play in the mechanism of fermentation; and, second, that the transformation is not a
simple breaking-down of the molecules of sugar into the
molecules of alcohol and carbon dioxide, but a succession of
breakings-down, that the "conversion of sugar into alcohol
and carbon dioxide during the process of fermentation is
most probably the result of a series of reactions, during
which various intermediate products are momentarily
formed and then used up in the succeeding state of the
process." [4]

The fermentation that takes place in grape must is of
course much more involved than that which takes place in
controlled laboratory experiments, since the composition of

[4] Arthur Harden: *Alcoholic Fermentation,* p. 109. See also Amerine
and Joslyn: *Table Wines,* pp. 288 ff.

the must not only is variable but includes many other substances besides sugar and water, some of which undergo change along with the fermentation. The nature of these accessory changes—and it is these, after all, that are responsible for the infinite variety of wines—is still far from being perfectly understood. Vinous fermentation, furthermore, is only one of many different kinds of fermentation. Grapes when crushed into the fermenter carry on their skins a large population of organisms in which the true wine yeast is a distinct minority. These other organisms are yeasts and bacteria of numerous species, some of which are benign so far as alcoholic fermentation is concerned, but some of which may cause fermentations that are harmful or even completely destructive. There are ways of dealing with these aggressors, as we shall see. But the process of fermentation in wine-making may be summed up nevertheless as a struggle between the good yeasts, which seek to transform the must into wine, and those bad organisms which seek to prevent the successful transformation.

The family of the *Saccharomyces* is the one to which all good wine yeasts belong. Of these, three species in particular (*S. apiculatus, S. pastorianus*, and *S. ellipsoideus*) are conspicuous in vinous fermentation. The division of labor between these species is a matter of continuing investigation, but *S. ellipsoideus* is by common agreement the workhorse of the team. The spores of this yeast hibernate in the ground during the winter, but as summer advances they get about a good deal, being carried hither and thither by insects, birds, and the dust of every vagrant breeze. As the grapes ripen, the yeasts are deposited upon the grapeskins in great numbers; so that when the grapes are crushed, these yeasts, in company with other organisms, are abundantly present in a medium favorable to their rapid propagation. Normally [5] the conditions are more favorable to propagation of the wine yeasts than of the other organisms. The yeasts begin immediately to grow and to reproduce themselves by budding and separating, so that in a short time their number has increased beyond all belief. A single drop of the must contains thousands of them. The sugar of the grape juice, in the presence of the zymase which the yeast cells secrete, thereupon undergoes that involved series of reactions which ends only when each molecule of sugar has been transformed into almost equal quantities of alcohol and carbon dioxide. Pasteur gives the following estimate of what happens to each 100 grams of sugar:

	grams
Alcohol	48.4
Carbon dioxide	46.6
Glycerin	3.2
Succinic acid	.6
To the yeast	1.2
	100.0

There are slight quantities of many other substances. And the proportions at the end of fermentation are altered by the fact that a certain fraction of the alcohol escapes during fermentation.[6] But for practical purposes it is sufficiently accurate to say that a given quantity of sugar yields ap-

[5] I.e., when the grapes are sound and ripe and not deficient in acidity, when temperature is moderate, and when ordinary sanitary precautions are observed.

[6] As red wine ferments more rapidly and at a higher temperature than white, there is in red wine a slightly greater loss of alcohol during fermentation.

proximately equal quantities by weight of alcohol and carbon dioxide. The glycerin and succinic acid contribute to the softness and "body" of the finished wine.

Each cell of yeast is a separate factory, so to speak, for the production of these materials. The more cells there are, the more swiftly and surely a sound fermentation takes place and the less danger there is of interference by the dangerous organisms. Thus the wine-maker does what he can to assure a rapid multiplication of the good yeasts at the very start of fermentation.

5: YEAST INSURANCE

The old empirical method of assuring a rapid multiplication of yeast takes advantage (though the empiricists do not necessarily know it) of the fact that yeasts behave quite differently in the presence of an abundant supply of air and when air is denied them. When they have plenty of air, the yeasts reproduce themselves with lavish speed and vigor, but make little alcohol; when air is denied them, they do not reproduce themselves so rapidly, but their efficiency as makers of alcohol is greatly increased. That is why during crushing (or the more primitive treading) the grapes are given maximum contact with the air, and that is why the must is always exposed to the air during the first part of fermentation (but lightly covered, of course, to keep out flies and dust). That also justifies the old practice in the Bordeaux region of throwing the crushed grapes into the air with wooden shovels before placing them in the fermenting-vat.

Yeasts are also sensitive to heat and cold. Though they can exist at extremely low temperatures, they do not usually show signs of activity unless the temperature is at least 60° F., and they do their best work between 65° and 80° F. As the temperature rises above that point, they become still more active, but beyond 98° F. the rate of the production of alcohol becomes progressively slower, stopping entirely at about 105° F. If this heat is maintained for from forty minutes to an hour or more, they are killed; at still higher temperatures they die more quickly—in ten minutes at 140° F. All this should be slightly qualified, however, for different strains of yeast react differently and it is possible to "train" (actually, to select) a strain to work at unusually low or high temperatures—a fact of most importance in hot countries such as central California. In contrast to the temperate habits of the yeasts, the harmful bacteria that induce sickness in the wines are positively tropical in their preferences. Their liveliest activity begins at temperatures in which the saccharomyces begin to slow down. Consequently wine-makers exert every effort to keep their must at a temperature which allows the maximum activity of the good yeasts, but discourages that of the harmful bacteria— that is, between 65° and 80° F.

It makes little difference to the saccharomyces whether the must is acid or neutral. But the harmful bacteria require a neutral or only barely acid must for their vigorous development. Therefore if the must is sufficiently acid, they are held at bay, and the field is open for the yeasts.

Wine-makers, then, encourage the rapid development of the yeasts in every possible way—by aerating the must, by controlling its temperature, by seeing that it is not deficient in acidity. In this effort to make absolutely sure that the yeasts get a good start many wine-makers go still farther by adding vigorous yeast cultures—called *pieds de cuve* in France, *starters* in the United States. These are usually made by selecting a small quantity of sound, well-ripened grapes a few days in advance and seeing that they are in full and strong fermentation at the time of the main vintage. A quantity of this actively fermenting mixture, in which the yeasts are multiplying with great vigor, is then added to each vat of fresh must. A technically more elegant way of preparing starters—the one used in most large wineries —is to isolate with the help of a microscope a culture of pure yeast at the end of a successful fermentation and to preserve this dormant culture throughout the year in a refrigerator; just before the vintage this culture is added to a quantity of fresh, sterilized must, and its rapid development encouraged. A pure culture of this kind eliminates all chance that the bad ferments might develop along with the good in the starter. It also enables the wine-maker to select and perpetuate exactly the strain of yeast which has worked well for him in the past. An important recent development is the industrial production of a fine strain of wine yeast, which may be bought in dehydrated form.

6: SULPHUR AND ITS VIRTUES

Where wine-making has advanced technically to the point of using yeast starters it is now customary to carry the procedure one step farther. This is done by joining to the use of starters some means of inhibiting or destroying the miscellaneous ferments that are present naturally in the must.

The agent now generally used for this purpose is the gas called sulphur dioxide in one of its several readily available forms; and the process is known as "sulphuring."

Sulphur dioxide, or SO_2,[7] is the acrid gas that is formed by combination with oxygen when sulphur is burned. It is antiseptic, and the practice of burning sulphur wicks or candles in empty cooperage, to keep it sterile, is an ancient one. But it was not until modern times that the great versatility of this gas, as a tool in the hands of the wine-maker, came to be appreciated. As a fumigant for casks and barrels it is as valuable as ever. But it now has many other things to do, since, from the wine-maker's standpoint, it has two altogether remarkable qualities. First, it is a *selective* antiseptic or disinfectant which, when added to fresh must in appropriate doses, is capable of retarding or destroying the *bad* ferments without injuring the *good* yeasts. Second, it is an antioxidant, or reducing agent, capable of hindering the undesirable oxidation, or browning, of must or wine.

We see, then, the sort of role that sulphur dioxide can play at the beginning of fermentation. As soon as the grapes are crushed, they receive a dose of it. This swiftly kills the dangerous ferments but only temporarily stuns the good ones. Then after a brief interval the sterilized must is aerated by stirring or pumping. This revives the good yeasts, which promptly get to work. Or immediately after aeration the must is seeded with a yeast starter. At the same time, acting as a reducing agent, the SO_2 has prevented the brownish discoloration, accompanied by an "off" flavor, which can occur by oxidation, especially in the musts of

[7] Not to be confused with hydrogen sulphide (H_2S), with its odor of rotten eggs.

white wines, and more especially when the grapes are not in first-class condition.[8]

Another characteristic of SO_2 is that its free, or active, form conveniently disappears when it has done its work— by evaporation and in other ways. That part which remains behind in the wine exists, unnoticed and inoffensive, in what is called the "combined" state. It goes without saying that the excessive use of SO_2, and the use of it at the wrong times, are as bad as the excessive or untimely use of anything else. Too much SO_2, for example, can prevent all fermentation, even by the good yeasts; and in a finished wine too much SO_2 harms both bouquet and flavor and in really massive doses may actually be injurious to health. It is a fallacy, in short, to assume that because a little SO_2 may be a good thing, a great deal of SO_2 is an even better thing. Like all good things, including wine itself, its use should not be abused.

It is in wine-growing regions such as southern France, Algeria, and California (where musts are normally low in acidity and most liable to be troubled by defective fermentations) that the use of SO_2 to obtain a clean fermentation is most necessary. In regions where the must is normally well-supplied with acidity—in northern Europe or in eastern United States—the risk of a defective fermentation is far less. Nine times out of ten an entirely spontaneous fermentation yields sound wine.

There are several sources of SO_2. The burning of sulphur wicks or pastilles, though it remains the standard method of sterilizing cooperage, is not a practical way of sulphuring

---

[8] Compare the brownish discoloration of freshly cut apples and peaches that have been allowed to stand briefly.

must. For this purpose, the larger wineries employ the compressed, liquid SO_2 which comes in cylinders. But the simplest and best source of SO_2 for the small winery or the amateur wine-maker is the salt known as potassium metabisulphite ($K_2S_2O_5$). This is to be had as a white, crys-

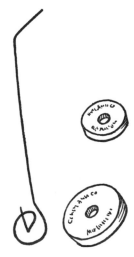

Sulphur pastilles with piece of No. 20 wire bent to receive and lower them into cask for burning.

talline powder soluble in water. It keeps well in a closed glass or plastic container. This salt, which is called "meta" for short in the wineries, contains 57 per cent by weight of SO_2, which is released when the salt is introduced into must or wine.

For practical purposes, then, a given weight of potassium metabisulphite provides one half its weight in SO_2. If, for example, *one gram* of SO_2 should be the correct dose for a given quantity of must, all one has to do is to add *two grams* of potassium metabisulphite, dissolved in a bit of warm water, and stir thoroughly. The correct dose of the gas is instantly released, as your nose will inform you. The advantage of this technique lies not only in its accuracy and simplicity but in the fact that nothing else is added to the must which would not normally be found there, the other products of the reaction that releases the sulphur-dioxide gas being trifling quantities of water and small quantities of cream of tartar, both normal constituents of must.[9]

7: THE FERMENTATION

After the wine-maker has prepared the way for a favorable fermentation (and we will assume in what follows that red wine is being made), very little time elapses before the must in the vat begins to show definite signs of activity. Soon there is the distinct and delicious odor of fermentation about the open mouth of the vat, and a gentle gurgle is heard. The must begins to heave, like the lava of a restive volcano, and the solid matter of the grapes rises to the surface, forming what the French call the *chapeau*, or hat. If a hole is poked through the chapeau, the liquid beneath bubbles and foams up through. Fermentation is under way. Steadily it gathers force; the gurgling becomes louder until it sounds like the hum of swarming bees, the chapeau more densely packed, the odor of the gas more insistent, so that if it is breathed directly it produces a sharp, choking sensation. In large wineries which do not have forced-draft ventilation, there are strict rules against approaching the

[9] Sodium metabisulphite is sometimes used for this same purpose, but ought not to be.

vats without permission, and people have been suffocated to death by the gas; for it is heavier than air and gradually displaces it from the floor up. Persons entering a poorly ventilated fermenting-cellar when violent fermentation is under way usually carry a lighted candle, which goes out if the gas is too thick for safety.

The systems of *cuvage*—that is, the actual conduct of the fermentation—differ from one wine-making region to another. In most, the "open" system is employed, by which the chapeau floats unimpeded on the surface of the fermenting must. When this method is used, the chapeau is broken up at least twice a day with a wooden spade or special "punchers" and thoroughly mixed with the liquid beneath it. This is called "punching down"; and it is done partly because the yeasts develop more rapidly at the surface and it is desirable to distribute them evenly throughout the whole fermenting mass, and partly to allow all of the liquid an even contact with the skins, which contain the coloring matter. In Burgundy the wine-makers used to break up the chapeau by stripping off their clothes, climbing onto the solid mass, and gradually working their way down into it, where they thrashed about until they were completely exhausted or could stand the fumes no longer. This method may be, and has been, criticized quite freely on sanitary, æsthetic, and humanitarian grounds, and I do not know that it is still used anywhere. But the amateur usually punches down by rolling up his sleeves and stirring the mass with his arms. When wine is fermented in enormous quantities, punching down is obviously impossible. The same result is accomplished by the process called "pumping over": free-run juice is drawn off through a valve at the base of the fermenting-tank and pumped back at the top.

During the fermentation the temperature of the must rises considerably—more in a large tank than in a small one (because a large tank has a smaller proportionate area of radiating surface) and more in a concrete tank than in a wooden one (because concrete allows still less radiation). Thus small wooden or stainless-steel or plastic fermenters are superior. In a careful fermentation, the frequent taking of the temperature of the must is as much a routine practice as in a hospital. If it threatens to rise above the danger point, at which the good yeasts grow sluggish and the bad ferments become active, heroic measures are taken to bring the temperature down. Coils are submerged in the fermenting mass and cold water or a refrigerant pumped through them. Or (this is the preferred practice in California) the fermenting wine is drawn off at the bottom and pumped through a stainless-steel heat exchanger, of the kind used in dairies, and back into the tank. Wine-makers who proceed on a less technological plane devise a rough-and-ready method of cooling, the favorite in some areas being to heave in a few cakes of ice if the must contains enough sugar to stand the dilution, or simply to trust to luck and a prompt turn in the weather.

A sudden drop in temperature, if great enough, can be troublesome to the wine-maker, though it is not nearly so dangerous to the wine as a rise.

If the fermentation goes forward smoothly, with no such trying interludes, the violence begins presently to subside. The humming is reduced to a whisper, and the chapeau, hitherto held up by the force of the gas rising through the must, begins to sink to the bottom. Wine-makers measure

the progress of the fermentation by means of a saccharometer, the same instrument with which the sugar content
of the must is measured before fermentation begins. The
saccharometer, known also among wine-makers as a "stem"
or "spindle," is a very simple and inexpensive little instrument that every wine-maker ought to own. More about it
later.

When the fermentation (of red wine) is "normal," the
sugar is transformed into alcohol at the rate of perhaps four
per cent a day; so that a must of twenty per cent sugar is
fermented out dry in about five days. But the period may
vary from three to ten days. Then it is time to think of
drawing off and pressing. The precise moment for pressing
is a matter of individual preference or regional custom. In
the Bordeaux district the unpressed wine used to be left on
its *marc* [1] sometimes for several weeks after the violent fermentation had finished, though the practice is rare now.
The Burgundians, on the other hand, have a saying: the
quicker the fermentation, the better the wine; and they
make haste to separate the new wine from its marc at the
earliest possible opportunity. In the United States the customary practice, both in California and in the Eastern
wineries, is to draw down and press when the must still
contains a small quantity of unfermented sugar, allowing
the fermentation to finish at a more leisurely pace in the
storage containers.

In pressing, the bulk of the new wine is allowed to drain
from the pomace. When all has drained that is going to
drain, the saturated mass that remains is transferred to the
press. The pomace, after pressing, is loosened and stirred

---

[1] The solid residue, also called pomace.

about with a wood-tined pitchfork or other appropriate implement and given another pressing. The pomace may then be set aside either for the making of sugar wine or *piquette,* or for distillation. In some regions the pomace fresh from the press is used as fodder for draft animals. Ordinarily, when ready to be discarded, it goes into a compost pile or back to the vineyard as a top dressing for the soil. Distillation of thoroughly pressed pomace yields a fiery and indelicate spirit.[2]

After the pressing the new wine is transferred to casks or other containers in which, during a gentle secondary fermentation, all remaining traces of sugar are eliminated and the wine undergoes the changes that transform it from a liquid which is merely alcoholic into something really worth the trouble.

The foregoing description of fermentation was based on the production of red wine. The course of fermentation in the making of white wine is different in two ways: (1) the grapes are *pressed immediately* after crushing, and the resulting fresh, sweet juice is fermented out of contact with the skins; and (2) the course of fermentation is much slower. Details of procedures for red wine and white wine are dealt with in Chapters VIII and IX respectively.

[2] Called *marc* in France and *grappa* in Italy. Amateur distillation is strictly illegal in the United States.

CHAPTER VII

Layout and Equipment

The amateur must fit his wine-making labors into whatever space he has. If he is lucky enough to live in the country, he may be able to adapt a part of a farm building to his needs; if a city dweller, he will make do with laundry, basement, or garage or even, *in extremis*, a corner of the kitchen or pantry. Following are some notes on the desirable conditions for wine-making. The potential wine-maker must work out his own compromises.

A concrete floor with a drain in it is advantageous, because crushing and pressing are messy operations; and running water, preferably hot and cold, should be near at hand. In small-scale wine-making, the simplest solution of the clean-up problem is often to do the crushing and pressing on the back porch or in the back yard. It should be possible to hold the temperature of the fermenting-room at around 65°–70° F. during the vintage period and, ideally, into early December. Basement temperatures are usually satisfactory, except next to the oil burner. If an outbuilding is to be used, it should be sufficiently insulated, and in cold climates should have some source of heat, as for instance a small stove or portable electric heater. When the lingering traces of fermentation are finished (say by December), colder temperature is desirable for clearing and stabilizing the wine, though not indispensable. A temperature as low as 25° F. maintained for several weeks is by no means harmful to the new wine. The Eastern wineries obtain this by throwing open the doors of their primary storage cellars. In addition, the wine-maker should consider such matters as ventilation, excessive humidity or excessive dryness, lighting, storage space for wine-making equipment as well as wine itself, and sanitation (wine is sensitive stuff, easily contaminated and liable to pick up strong odors if exposed to them). The wine-maker will also want a place for tasting and testing and for the safekeeping of his records, preferably near a sink or basin. Most domestic wine-makers use the kitchen, and a corner of a kitchen shelf.

If expansion from purely domestic wine-making to small-scale commercial production is contemplated, innumerable mistakes are avoided by consulting with one who has been through the mill, and a copy of the Federal Regulations must be obtained [1] and studied. State authorities must also be consulted.

ESSENTIAL EQUIPMENT

Most domestic wine-makers ferment between twenty and one hundred gallons a year, using grapes of their own growing or grapes bought in the market. Smaller quantities

[1] Obtainable from the nearest office of the Alcohol, Tobacco and Firearms Division, Internal Revenue Service, Treasury Department.

may be successfully made,[2] but twenty to forty gallons require hardly more labor than five gallons. Whatever the quantity to be made, certain items are necessary:

1. *Small crusher*
2. *Small wine or cider press*
3. *Saccharometer*
4. *Pails (two necessary, three desirable)*
5. *Tub*
6. *Fermenting-vat*
7. *Funnel*
8. *Storage containers (glass bottles or oak cooperage)*
9. *Rubber tube*
10. *Corker*
11. *Absorbent cotton*
12. *Sulphur pastilles and metabisulphite*
13. *Two-pint Pyrex measure*

Crusher. The usual small crusher consists of a hopper and pair of wooden or aluminum meshing rollers that are turned by a crank and flywheel. Grapes are placed in the hopper and crushed through the rollers directly into tub or fermenter. Most winery crushers operate on the same principle but are heavier and power-operated. In commercial operations the crushed grapes are usually passed through a device that removes them from the stems.

Press. One may begin with a small second-hand cider press. The type of hand press illustrated is inexpensive and is built in sizes ranging from 14 to 30 inches in diameter. Larger screw presses of the same type, but with various

[2] At Boordy Vineyard we have made experimental batches as small as one pint.

ratchet, lever, and hydraulic-jack devices for increasing pressure, are used throughout Europe.

Hand crusher.

Saccharometer. This, with accompanying hydrometer jar, is essential. The wine-maker must know the sugar content of his grapes, since alcoholic content of finished wine is related directly to it.[3] The saccharometer is the device for measuring sugar content and so telling the wine-maker where he stands. It is a glass spindle, weighted at one end so that it will float upright in the juice to be tested. It is, in fact, a special form of hydrometer, and what it does is to measure the specific gravity of the juice. A liquid containing dissolved sugar and other solids is heavier than water and thus causes the saccharometer to float higher than it would in plain water. If the hydrometer jar is filled with plain water, the instrument will come to rest so that zero

[3] Remember the ratio: 2 degrees of sugar equal 1 per cent of alcohol.

on the scale is exactly at the level of the fluid. If the juice contains, say, 20 per cent of sugar, then the instrument, floating much higher, will give an appropriate reading at the level of the liquid. It is as simple as that.

Hand press, available in various sizes.

Saccharometers are made in various sizes (the longer the spindle, the more accurate the reading), and they are fitted with scales that differ according to the convention of the country. In the United States the Brix or Balling scale (they are different names for the same thing) is used by most wine-makers. This scale gives a direct reading of the proportion by weight of "total solids" in the must; and of course most of these "total solids" are sugar. French wine-makers, on the other hand, prefer a scale that indicates the

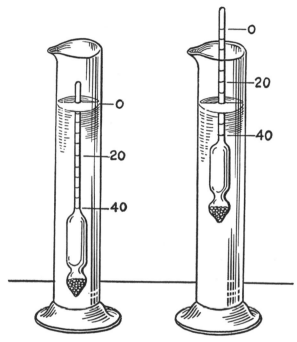

In plain water (left) saccharometer sinks to point 0. In grape juice containing 24 per cent sugar, saccharometer floats at 24 on the scale.

potential alcoholic content of wine to be made from a given sample. The Germanic countries use still another, the Oechsle scale. The French scale is simplest to use; but all these scales are referable to the specific gravity of the juice. Saccharometers are to be had from dealers in laboratory or optical instruments as well as from winery supply houses. They are inexpensive.

Pails and Tub. Grape juice and wine are mildly acid and hence interact with most metals. Ordinary white enameled pails, 12-quart size, are inexpensive and satisfactory, but should be discarded when (or if) much of the enamel chips off; stainless-steel or plastic dairy pails are ideal. As for the tub, it should be of wood or plastic. Two good tubs of 25-gallon capacity may be made in about five minutes by sawing a second-hand barrel in two. The interior surface of such tubs should be scraped and scrubbed and then coated (using a cheap new paintbrush) with melted household paraffin. Before being used, they should be soaked tight; the paraffin coating may be renewed as needed.

Funnel. This should be of good size and should be enameled or made of heavily tinned copper, stainless steel or plastic.

Fermenting-Vat. For domestic operations, a good fermenter is easily made by knocking out one of the heads of a second-hand 50-gallon barrel. This is done by driving off the two top hoops with a hammer and blunt cold chisel or a grooved cooper's hammer. The head, thus loosened, is knocked into the barrel with a mallet and pulled out edgewise, after which the hoops are replaced and driven tight. The interior is then scraped and brushed clean and given a coating of hot paraffin. Before being used, the fermenter should be soaked tight. A 50-gallon fermenter of this type will take 7 or 8 bushels of grapes at a time. At Boordy Vineyard, for small commercial production, we use a battery of fermenters of this type, but made of 185-gallon second-hand Spanish casks of the kind in which olives are shipped to this country. They hold about one-half ton of crushed grapes apiece, and are kept going all during the vintage season, being emptied and refilled every four or five days as the grapes come in. Large wineries use tanks of redwood, lined concrete or mild steel, stainless steel and fiberglass in large sizes.

Wine Containers. The novice wine-maker will do well in the beginning to use 5-gallon glass bottles, of the kind used for transporting chemicals or spring water. They are easily cleaned, they may be used interchangeably for white wine or red, they cannot deteriorate in storage (though they can be broken), they allow the novice to see what is happening, and they are easily moved about even when full. For a 20-gallon vintage, the wine-maker will require, not 4, but 5 of these bottles—a spare. He will also want a few bottles of smaller sizes—a 3-gallon, a 2-gallon, and several 1-gallon bottles—to take care of fractional quantities.

The traditional storage material, however, is white-oak cooperage, which ranges in size from five-gallon kegs through barrels, butts, puncheons, bilge casks, and ovals on up to great tanks holding many thousands of gallons. Storage in oak cooperage is undeniably advantageous for red wines (though not for white); but the use of sizes smaller than fifty gallons involves much loss through evaporation, the risk of excessive oakiness in the flavor of the wine, leakage, and many other hazards. Even in the larger sizes, oak cooperage is temperamental material, requiring constant attention. When empty, it is subject to shrinkage, warping, mold spoilage, and dry rot. Hoops deteriorate rapidly in humid locations. Cooperage is hard to clean and keep clean, must be skillfully conditioned before any wine at all is put into it, springs sudden and inexplicable leaks,

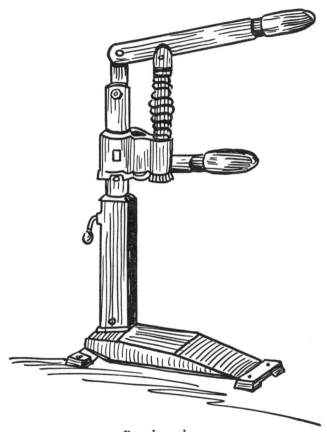

Bench corker.

and cannot be used interchangeably for red and white wine. The amateur is well advised to steer clear of cooperage until he is thoroughly aware of what he is doing and has made sure of the availability of a competent cooper. Except for the aging of the very best red wines, the trend wherever wine is made is away from the use of small oak cooperage.

Rubber Tube. This should be a six-foot length of good-quality laboratory tubing, ⅜" or ½" inside diameter. It is

Small hand corker.

used for racking (that is, siphoning) the young wine at the various stages of its development and also for siphoning from storage into wine bottles when the wine is finished and ready to be bottled and binned away. The intake end should be notched, to allow free suction.

Corker. Straight-sided wine corks must be inserted into the neck of the bottle with a special device, since their diameter is considerably larger than the inside diameter of the neck. A hand corker and a bench corking machine are illustrated. Other inexpensive types of hand corking machines are to be had.

Miscellaneous. Uses of metabisulphite and sulphur pastilles (or sulphur strips) have been mentioned already and will be returned to farther on. The Pyrex measure will be found useful in many ways. Absorbent cotton is needed for wadding the mouths of five-gallon bottles.

NON-ESSENTIAL EQUIPMENT

The novice wine-maker can safely skip the next few pages for the time being. But after he has made wine successfully once or twice and has begun to get the feel of the wine-making art, he will begin to cast about for ways of saving labor and of improving control of actual wine-making procedures. The following notes may prove to be helpful when that point is reached. Many items of equipment are desirable even though not necessary, and some of the practices of large-scale wine-making can often be adapted to small-scale wine-making by exercising a bit of ingenuity.

Laboratory Equipment. The saccharometer, as we have seen, is a *sine qua non*. A large part of the world's wine is made with the assistance of no other testing device than this and perhaps a thermometer. But the meticulous and inquisitive wine-maker soon wants to make certain other tests besides that for sugar content. He wants to know the *total acidity* of the must before fermentation, of the new wine, and of the wine as it ages. Later on he may also want to test his wines for *volatile acidity*. Still later on he will want to make tests for both free and combined SO_2, especially if he takes to making sweet wines. For these purposes he needs a few pieces of relatively simple laboratory equipment, consisting of a titrating set plus the necessary reagents.

He is likely to want, presently, to know the precise *alcoholic content* of the wines he makes. For this purpose he will need a laboratory alembic, or distilling outfit, with accompanying alcohol hydrometer. In connection with this he will require a spirit lamp or small gas burner, a sink with running water, and various odds and ends of equipment such as a small plastic funnel, beakers, and graduated flasks.

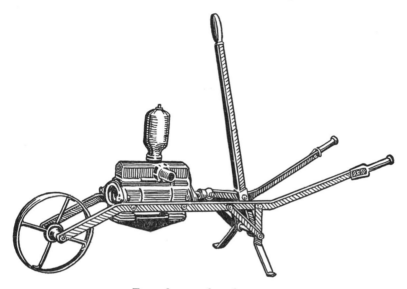

French type hand pump.

Such material may be picked up bit by bit—or, if the wine-maker is lucky, he may be able to acquire some of the in-genious small testing kits that have been developed in France and Germany for making these basic tests quickly and easily.

For the experimentally inclined, there is of course no limit to the range of laboratory work that may be done in connection with wine-making; but that sort of thing is be-yond the scope of this modest treatise.

Transfer Devices. Buckets, funnel, and rubber tubing

give way to more pretentious equipment when the scale of operations increases. Wineries use plunger pumps and centrifugal pumps for transferring freshly crushed grapes, stems and all. For small commercial production at Boordy Vineyard we use a French hand pump for this purpose, but for wine (rather than fresh must) we fall back on a ¾-inch

Small stop-start bottle filler, to be attached to end of racking tube.

bronze mail-order gear pump mounted on a homemade base and driven by a ¼-h.p. motor, which pumps at the rate of about 5 gallons a minute, with ¾-inch dairy hose. Stainless steel is preferable to bronze, but much more expensive; pumps that expose iron to the wine must never be used.

Filtration. For many years the use of filters in wine-making was considered a heresy, and in small-scale wine-making the traditional method of clarification by fining [4] is still en-

[4] Discussed in Chapter XI.

tirely adequate. Furthermore, primitive methods of filtration in which the wine is exposed freely to air while being filtered (as through filter paper or a bag filter) should never be used. In commercial wine-making, however, clari-

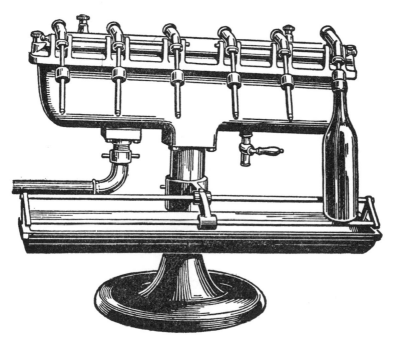

Six-bottle siphon filler.

fication by pumping wine through properly designed filters is now widely practiced. The experimentally inclined may be tempted by one or another of the small laboratory-size pad filters that are on the market; but they are expensive, and for small-scale wine-making they are a distinct luxury.

Miscellaneous. As time goes on, the wine-maker will feel

the need for various other small items, some of which are listed here for the record: a supply of clean old cloths, a graduated glass for making blends, a roll of wax paper and a box of paper tissues, rubber stoppers in various sizes, fermentation valves, bronze or wooden spigots, a stop-start device for use on the end of his rubber tube when bottling, a bench or wall corkscrew, a bottle-rinsing device (this may be attached to an ordinary water faucet), scrub brushes, bottle brush with long wire handle, wire brush for removing rust from barrel hoops, galvanized tub for soaking bottles, rubber gloves, card index for keeping records of vintage data, hanging meat scales or platform scale for weighing grapes, wooden spade or shovel for handling pomace, dolly with rubber casters for moving filled tubs or five-gallon bottles, heavy wooden mallet, bung starter, and "wine thief" for taking samples.

CHAPTER VIII

How to Make Red Wine

We will assume that red-wine grapes are ripe on the vines and ready to pick, or that a supply has been arranged for.[1] What follows assumes a domestic vintage of modest size, using a fifty-gallon barrel as a vat. Since the fifty-gallon vat is the limiting factor, the maximum quantity of grapes to be handled at any one time is seven good bushels or twelve California "lugs" (the standard California shipping box).

Crushing. Check the fermenter for cleanness and tightness (it should be tightened several days in advance by soaking and driving down hoops). Mount the fermenter on three bricks or short pieces of two-by-four. Place the crusher directly across the open top of the fermenter. Empty grapes into the hopper and turn the crank. The crushed bunches, dripping juice, will plop directly into the vat. Do not wash the grapes in advance. Keep an eye

[1] The Californian will be using vinifera varieties exclusively, bought in the market, bought direct from a known source, or grown himself. The Easterner may buy the ordinary California varieties shipped in by refrigerated car or, if he grows his own, may use either the standard American sorts or some of the new French hybrids. Full particulars on grape varieties are to be found in Appendix A.

out for badly rotted bunches, but it is not necessary to inspect each berry. The grapes need not be stemmed. Fill the fermenter no more than three-fourths full.

When the crushing is done, rinse the crusher immediately and clean things up. Then remove a tumblerful of juice and set it aside to use in testing for sugar content and possibly for total acidity. (If you want to, remove a milk-bottleful and put it in the refrigerator; the sediment will settle overnight, and in the morning you will have fresh grape juice for breakfast, something that few Americans know anything about.) After the sample has been removed, add to the remainder a dose of potassium metabisulphite dissolved in a tumblerful of hot water, and stir in thoroughly. *Correct dose:* ⅛ oz. (3.5 gm.) per 100 lb. of grapes. When the "meta" has been stirred in, cover the open top of the fermenter with a clean cloth to keep out dust and fruit flies. (Most wine-makers using Eastern grapes do not bother with the "meta" dose, but depend on the natural acidity of the must to keep the vintage healthy. When California grapes are used, the "meta" dose is important.)

ANALYZING AND CORRECTING THE MUST

Next, test the sample that has been drawn off, and if necessary correct the must. All wine-makers test for sugar content; the test for acidity is not absolutely necessary and few amateur wine-makers bother with it.

Testing for Sugar. Experience has shown that a finished table wine, to be stable and palatable, should have an alcoholic content of from 10 to 12 per cent by volume. Thus, if the juice of the freshly crushed grapes is too low in sugar content to achieve this proportion of alcohol, it should be

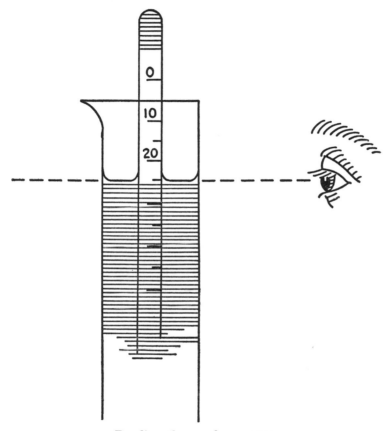

Reading the saccharometer.

corrected by an appropriate addition of sugar before fermentation. In testing the sugar content, use either a Balling or a French-type (Dujardin-Salleron) saccharometer. Strain the sample of must to be tested through a clean piece

WHAT THE SACCHAROMETER SHOWS			TO MAKE WINE OF 10% BY VOL.‡ add		TO MAKE WINE OF 12% BY VOL.‡ add	
Crude Ball-ing *	Potential Alcohol (Dujardin scale) †	Sugar per gal. (in lb.)	In pounds per 10 gal.	In ounces per gal.	In pounds per 10 gal.	In ounces per gal.
10	4.5	.6875	7.426	11.80	10.125	16.19
11	5.1	.7765	6.436	10.13	9.234	14.77
12	5.7	.8663	5.539	8.86	8.337	13.33
13	6.2	.9568	4.634	7.41	7.432	11.90
14	7.2	1.0480	3.722	5.94	6.521	10.43
15	7.8	1.1399	2.903	4.64	5.601	8.92
16	8.4	1.2326	1.876	3.00	4.675	7.47
17	9.2	1.3260	.942	1.50	3.740	5.98
18	9.8	1.4202			2.798	4.31
19	10.5	1.5151			1.849	2.95
20	11.2	1.6106			.894	1.42
21	11.9	1.7073				
22	12.6	1.8047				
23	13.4	1.9027				
24	14.1	2.0016				
25	14.9	2.1014				
26	15.5	2.2020				

* The indication when the Balling saccharometer is floated in grape juice. It indicates the proportion by weight of total solids (most of the solids being sugar).

† The indication when the French, or Dujardin, saccharometer is floated in grape juice. Direct reading shows potential alcoholic content by volume of the unfermented juice. May be used interchangeably with the Balling scale for the purpose of determining sugar content of juice and correcting.

‡ Remember that the result is not precise—the yield of alcohol varying under the conditions of fermentation. To make wine of 11% by volume, add quantity halfway between that for 10% wine and that for 12% wine.

of cheesecloth into a dish or cup and pour it into the hydrometer jar, which should be set on a level table. The temperature of the sample should be between 55° and 75° F. If higher or lower, cool it or warm it accordingly. Rinse and dry the saccharometer and insert it carefully, by the tip, into the sample. When it is floating freely and has come to rest, take a reading at the true surface of the liquid. When the reading is taken, refer to the table, "Testing and Correcting the Must." This will tell you whether the must needs sugar correction or not; and if it does, how much sugar is to be added.

EXAMPLE NO. 1. *The reading shows 20° on the Balling or 11.2° on the Dujardin-Salleron scale. Referring to the table, we see that no correction is required.*

EXAMPLE NO. 2. *The reading shows 16° on the Balling scale or 8.4° on the Dujardin-Salleron. Refer to the table. To make a wine of 10 per cent alcohol by volume add 3 oz. of sugar per gallon of juice; to make a wine of 12 per cent by volume, add 7.47 oz. of sugar per gallon of juice.*

In making up a deficiency of sugar, use ordinary granulated sugar (sucrose). On being dissolved and mixed with the must, this is hydrolyzed immediately into grape sugar (dextrose and levulose), which is indistinguishable from that occurring naturally in the grapes. Such a correction of the natural deficiency of sugar is practiced (under appropriate restrictions, of course) in the most important wine-making regions of the world. The musts of the finest Burgundies are sugared when necessary, as are those of most German white wines. During the 1963 vintage, and again in 1968, when grapes ripened badly in France, sugaring (*sucrage* to the French) was extended to the Bordeaux region. If *sucrage* for the purpose of making up a natural deficiency is a sound practice for such wines as these, it is a sound practice in making American wines.

In correcting the red-wine must, assume that 12 lugs, or 7 bushels, will yield approximately 20 gallons of juice. Thus, using the table, compute the approximate amount of sugar to be added.

> EXAMPLE. *Suppose the saccharometer indicates 18° Balling or 9.8° Dujardin-Salleron. The table indicates that the correct amount of sugar to add is 4.31 oz. per gallon of must. Then 4.31 times twenty equals 86.20 oz. or 5.4 lb.—the proper amount of sugar to add.*

The sugar should be dissolved in a small quantity of the juice drawn from the vat specially for the purpose and warmed slightly. The dissolved sugar is then added to the vat and stirred thoroughly, in order that it be evenly distributed. It may be stirred with a clean wooden paddle or with well-washed arms. As the dose is based on an estimated rather than an exact measure of the amount of juice, the must should be tested again with the saccharometer after the sugar has been thoroughly mixed, in order to make sure that it now falls within proper limits of sugar content.

When the must is too sweet, as may sometimes happen when California grapes are used, it must be brought to normal by the addition of water—a dubious practice at best [2]—

[2] And strictly forbidden to commercial wineries in the United States should addition bring the acidity of the must below .5 grams per 100 cc. expressed as tartaric acid.

or blended with that of low-sugar grapes. Fortunately the must is seldom too sweet if the proper grapes are used. If water must be added for the purpose, plain city water is satisfactory except in regions where the local water supply is of poor quality—in which case use distilled water. After the water is added, the must should be tested once more with the saccharometer.

Determining Acidity. California grapes often have an acidity rather lower, and Eastern grapes an acidity rather higher, than the ideal. Despite this fact, most amateur wine-makers are content to test for sugar content alone, taking a chance that the acidity is satisfactory. But the test for total acidity, once the idea is grasped, is so simple that it can be done quickly even though the wine-maker knows little of chemistry. Although several different acids and their salts are normally present in the must, for wine-making purposes it is sufficient to know the *total acidity*, which is always expressed in terms of an acid of known strength, usually tartaric acid. Thus one says that a given must has a total acidity of .9 grams per 100 cc. expressed as tartaric. This is of course an arbitrary means of measurement—a unit of measure. What it really means to the chemist is that the total acidity of the must is such that the quantity of alkaline substance required to neutralize it is the same as would be necessary *if all the acid in the must were tartaric acid.* The known strength of any other acid would do as well for a unit of measure, but tartaric is the commonly accepted standard.

The classic method of determining total acidity is that of titration, which, as everyone who has studied any elementary chemistry knows, is simply the neutralization of an acid by a measured quantity of an alkaline solution of known strength. The following method, while not accurate

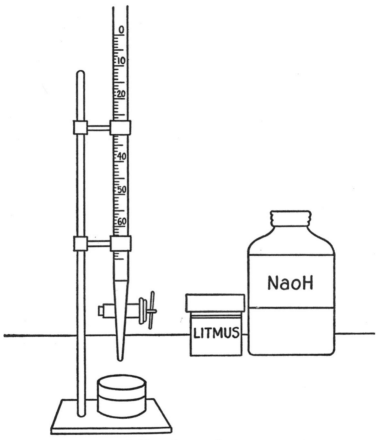

Acid-testing equipment.

enough for precise work, is entirely satisfactory for ordinary purposes in wine-making.

Procedure. The apparatus consists of (a) a *burette* graduated in cubic centimeters or milliliters (cc. or ml.), together with a stand to hold it upright; (b) a *pipette* for measuring fifteen ml.; (c) a small *beaker* or *cup*; (d) a small *glass rod* or plastic teaspoon for stirring; (e) an indicator, which for ordinary work may be a small bottle each of red and blue *litmus paper*; (f) titrating solution, which is *sodium hydroxide* one-fifth normal (NaOH N/5). Any druggist can make a pint of it for you. It should be well stoppered between tests. Be sure that the NaOH is N/5 and not some other concentration, such as N/10; for only N/5 will give proper results.

With the pipette, measure out exactly fifteen ml. of the strained must that is to be tested and place in the beaker or cup under the burette. Fill the burette with the sodium-hydroxide solution up to the point marked "O." Open the stopcock of the burette and allow a little of the sodium hydroxide to flow into the beaker or cup containing the sample under test, and stir with the glass rod. After each addition of NaOH, touch a strip of red and a strip of blue litmus paper with the tip of the rod. As long as the drop of liquid on the blue litmus paper causes it to turn red, and the red paper shows no change of color, the sample is still acid. Continue to add the NaOH to the must sample until the damp rod fails to turn the blue paper red and just barely tinges the red paper blue. The total acid of the sample has then been neutralized. If the red paper tests violently blue, then too much of the alkaline solution has been added to the must. The accuracy of the test depends on titrating exactly to neutrality. A bit of practice makes perfect, or *almost* perfect.

When the sample has been exactly neutralized, read the number of *ml.* indicated on the scale of the burette—the quantity, that is, which was used in the process of neutralizing the sample. This number gives *directly* the total acidity of the sample in grams per liter *as tartaric*.

> EXAMPLE. *If 8.5 ml. of the alkaline solution was required to neutralize the acid in the must, then the total acidity of the sample is 8.5 grams per liter as tartaric. Since it has become a convention in wine-making circles to express total acidity not in grams per liter but in grams per 100 cubic centimeters (i.e., one tenth of a liter), the result as given by the scale on the burette is brought into conformity with this practice by moving the decimal point one place to the left. That is to say, a total acidity of 8.5 grams per liter is the same as a total acidity of .85 grams per 100 cubic centimeters—or, for short, .85 per cent.*

Correcting Acidity. The acidity of California grapes ranges from about .4 to .8 per cent, as tartaric, and higher only rarely. The acidity of Eastern grapes ranges normally much higher—from .6 to 1.8, at the extremes. Wine technicians agree that good wine grapes ought to have an acidity of at least .8 and that on the other hand an acidity of more than 1.3 may in the end produce a rather harsh or green-tasting wine.

The advantage of a fairly high acidity as an aid to healthy fermentation has already been mentioned. Much of the harshness of the wine is tempered by time alone. Furthermore, as we shall see in the chapters dealing with the new wine, a substantial proportion of the acid in grapes of high acidity is malic acid; and one of the characteristics of malic acid is that, when the wine is aged under suitable conditions, it breaks down into a much less "sour" acid—namely, lactic acid. This occurs through the agency of the so-called malo-lactic fermentation, the tremendous importance of which in softening and improving wines made of high-acid grapes is only now coming to be fully realized. The effect of this breakdown of malic acid into lactic is frequently to cut the total effective acidity of a wine almost in two.[3] There are, however, at least three other methods of reducing the total acidity of a high-acid must: (1) by blending this must with the must of low-acid grapes; (2) by chemical deacidification; (3) by cutting with a solution of sugar and water.

The first of these three methods is the best, provided low-acid grapes are available. The second method is practical only after fermentation and consists in neutralizing a part of the wine's acidity by adding an alkaline salt, usually pure precipitated chalk. The use of chalk is tricky, however. Cutting high-acid must with a sugar-and-water solution is a traditional practice in the Eastern United States, but is tolerated only within certain definite limits for commercial wineries. Government regulations allow cutting up to one third of the volume of the original must, *provided* that in so doing the total acidity of the mixture of must and sugar solution is not brought below .5 acidity. The method is simply to prepare a solution of water and cane sugar in a concentration of about 20 degrees Balling,[4] add it to the must, and mix thoroughly. It goes without saying that cutting in this manner drastically alters the normal chemical constitution

[3] Reference to *effective* acidity ought logically to be followed by an exposition of the concept of pH, or hydrogen-ion concentration. But the introduction of the subject would only complicate matters for practical wine-makers without improving their wine.

[4] That is, a sugar solution of 1.70 lb. (27 oz.) per gallon. Dissolve sugar in half the quantity of water, then make up to quantity.

of the must, and results in a thinner and lighter-bodied wine.

As Eastern wine-makers are usually concerned about excessive acidity, so California wine-makers are more apt to be concerned about deficient acidity. In California, as in other hot winegrowing regions, it is accepted practice to increase the total acidity of a must that is deficient in acid by the addition of tartaric acid. When done with circumspection, this promotes a more reliable fermentation and improves the quality of the wine. In making red wine from California grapes, acidity may be adjusted to about .7 per cent. Adjustment of acidity should always be done *before* fermentation.

> EXAMPLE. *If the must tests .5 per cent total acidity, add 2.0 grams of pure tartaric acid per liter of juice. Assuming that the crushed grapes in the fermenter are to yield approximately 20 gallons of wine: 20 gallons equals 75.6 liters (1 gallon equals 3.78 liters), and 75.6 times 2.0 grams equals 151.2 grams (1 ounce equals 28.35 gm.). To add, merely dissolve the necessary weight of U.S.P. dry tartaric acid (to be had at any drugstore) in warm water, throw it in, and mix thoroughly.*

FERMENTATION

We now have in the fermenting-vat enough crushed grapes to fill it approximately three-quarters full. This must has been tested and if necessary adjusted for sugar content or acidity. It may also have had a preliminary purifying dose of potassium metabisulphite. The top of the vat is covered with a clean cloth. At the end of eight to twelve hours the cloth should be removed. If the must is not to be fermented

Open fermentation.

with the aid of a yeast starter, it should be thoroughly stirred at this time and the cloth replaced.

If the must is to be fermented with the aid of a yeast starter,[5] now is the time to add it and stir it in. Preparation

[5] More important if California grapes are used than if Eastern grapes are used.

of the starter should have begun about four days in advance of the crushing. Assuming dehydrated wine yeast, moisten contents of envelope with a bit of warm water, let stand until rehydrated, then mix into a quart of strained fresh grape juice and keep in a warm place until needed. Whether such a starter is used or not, the must should then be stirred morning and evening from this point on to the conclusion of fermentation. At the end of twenty-four hours the characteristic symptoms of fermentation should be evident. If fermentation is not apparent at the end of forty-eight hours, measures should be taken to stimulate it.

The cause of delayed fermentation is almost always low temperature.[6] The simplest cure, if the must is too cold, is to aerate it thoroughly by stirring and then fill a clean bucket full of fairly warm water and lower it gently into the must, securing it by means of a light rope to a strong stick or board placed across the top of the vat. The warm water should be renewed occasionally. Another method is to remove a pailful of the must and place the pail in a tub of fairly warm water until the must is well warmed; then pour the warmed must back into the vat. In commercial wineries the must is warmed by being circulated through heat exchangers, or else by inserting a coil into the vat, through which warm water is circulated.

When fermentation begins, skins and stems rise to the surface to form the chapeau. The whole contents of the vat indeed seem to swell. That is why the vat was filled only three-quarters full. Better to take this precaution than to have to cope with an overflow.

The chapeau should not be allowed to touch the cloth.

[6] Though an excessive dose of "meta" has the same effect.

If it does, and the cloth gets a damp stain, replace it with a clean one. It is a good thing to drill a number of holes in the barrel head that was removed in making the vat, and when the fermentation is going well, to place this over the open top of the vat as a loose cover, throwing the cloth over it. This keeps the cloth from sagging, and in cold weather helps to retain the heat of fermentation. It also helps to retain a cap of carbon dioxide over the top of the fermenting mass. This cap prevents the free access of air to the must, once the fermentation is well started. Remember that yeast multiplies best in the presence of air (during the first twenty-four or forty-eight hours of fermentation), but is more efficient in producing alcohol when not in the presence of air (during the remainder of the fermentation). Cloth and cover should be removed and the chapeau broken up every morning and evening during the whole period of fermentation.

The temperature of the must rises considerably during fermentation. It is advisable not to let it get above 90° F. The small-scale wine-maker may control fermentation temperature to some extent by controlling the temperature of the room. Removal of the cover helps to lower it.

The wine-maker should take a reading with a saccharometer each evening, when the chapeau is broken up. This will give a notion of the advance of the fermentation. It is only an approximate measure, however, for the steadily increasing proportion of alcohol renders the scale inaccurate. For example, when the fermenting must registers zero on the saccharometer, the must still contains about two per cent of sugar. A completely dry new wine tests *below* zero, of course, as it has a lower specific gravity than water.

THE PRESSING

Every wine-maker has his own notion as to the best time to press. A good rule is to press when the saccharometer gives a reading between 0° and 4°—that is, when the fermentation has begun to slacken off, but two to five per cent of sugar still remains in the must. Normally this time is reached after three or four days of fermentation. Prompt pressing helps to make a "soft" wine because it keeps the new wine from absorbing too much tannin from the stems. Those who like an astringent wine, such as Chianti, may obtain it by delaying the pressing for several days.

Preparing the Equipment. Scrub the press with a hot solution of washing soda and rinse well in warm and cold water. Wash the containers (five-gallon glass bottles in the case of the small vintage) with the same solution and rinse thoroughly. Wash the pails and the funnel.

Pressing Procedure. In the case of large vintages, the free-run wine is drawn off from an appropriate bung or spigot near the bottom of the fermenter, and only the residue is pressed. In the case of a small vintage, the mass of pomace and new wine is merely bailed[7] from the barrel directly into the basket of the press. Much of the new wine drains between the slats of the press basket and so into the pails, one being filled while the other is poured through the funnel into one of the five-gallon bottles. This process is repeated until the press basket is full of pomace. Then the

[7] A third pail, or a large enameled or aluminum saucepan, will do for this.

basket load of pomace is pressed, but not too rapidly. When all of the juice has been pressed out that will come, reopen the press basket, loosen up the pomace, and give another pressing. In working with a small vintage, mix the pressed wine with the free-run wine.

When the pressing is finished, the mouth of each five-gallon bottle, *filled full*, should be carefully wiped with a clean dry cloth or paper towel, and a plug of absorbent cotton wadded in. These bottles should not be corked, as the wine is still fermenting and corks will be promptly blown out. The absorbent cotton lets the gas out but does not let in impurities from the air.[8] Remember, all bottles must be full, since an air space in the bottle provides ideal conditions for the growth of harmful molds and bacteria on the surface of the wine. If the wine-maker winds up with a five-gallon bottle that is not quite full, he should transfer this last wine to bottles of smaller sizes, also filling them full. These smaller batches will be found useful later on.[9]

The containers of newly pressed wine are then set aside, preferably on a sturdy shelf, in a place where the temperature is uniform *and not too low*, until the time for the first racking.

The new wine is now made. During the process of fermentation, and especially at the time of pressing, the wine-maker will doubtless have tasted it. Unless he is forewarned, he will be disappointed. During the course of fermentation it will be sweetish, with a yeasty aftertaste. At the time of pressing it will still be faintly sweetish and will also be harsh

---

[8] The meticulous prefer fermenting-valves instead of absorbent cotton. A fermenting-valve is a loop of glass tubing with water in it, so designed that the gas bubbles out through the water, but air cannot get back in. Most small-scale wine-makers do not bother with them.

[9] See pages 151–2.

and raw; and in addition it will still be muddy with yeast and other suspended matter. But that need cause no alarm, for though the must has most definitely been transformed into wine, the wine will not be ready to drink until more has happened to it. Patience will have its reward.

Subsequent care of the new red wine is discussed in Chapters X and XI.

CHAPTER IX

How to Make White Wine

W hite wine is made of grapes that are pressed *before* fermentation. It is not fermented on the skins, as red wine is. As the coloring matter of most varieties is in the skins exclusively and is extracted only during fermentation, white wine may consequently be made from some varieties of dark grapes, if the skins are not left long in contact with the juice. The small-scale wine-maker, however, will be prudent to use only white or pink grapes for white wine until he has acquired a feeling for the art.

As with red-wine grapes, a distinction has to be made between the vinifera varieties of California and those grown in the East. Usually good California red-wine grapes are easier to come by than good California white-wine grapes. Discussion of specific varieties is reserved to Appendix A.[1]

[1] See page 243 et seq.

139

HOW TO PROCEED

Place the crusher over the wooden tub.[2] Pour the grapes into the hopper of the crusher. When the hopper is full, turn the crank and run the grapes through into the tub. When there is a tubful of freshly crushed grapes, transfer them, stems and all, to the basket of the press, and press immediately. The pressure should be applied slowly but steadily, and to the full pressure that the press is capable of. It is very important to press thoroughly because the juice of freshly crushed grapes is sluggish and syrupy, the cell structure of the berries is not completely broken in the crushing,[3] and the berries yield their juice reluctantly. Grapes of different varieties will be found to behave very differently in the press.

When the first pressing is finished, loosen and stir the pomace, and press again. In making white wine it is worth while to press a third time. The yield of all pressings should be mixed. When the pomace has yielded all of its juice, discard it, refill the press basket with another load, and repeat the process. Domestic wine-makers may wish to save the pomace for the making of "sugar wine," as described in Chapter XII. As fast as the buckets are filled with the fresh juice, they should be poured into the five-gallon bottles in which the juice is to ferment. The fermenting-containers should be filled only three-fourths full.[4]

When the pressing is finished, a sample of the must is set

[2] See page 112. Or even a galvanized washtub *provided the interior is given a coating of acid-resistant plastic paint,* or a plastic garbage pail.

[3] When red wine is made, the cell structure is broken down during the fermentation, and the subsequent pressing is relatively more easy.

[4] If a barrel is used for fermenting, keep a flashlight handy for checking on the amount of fill.

aside for testing. A light pre-fermentation dose of metabi-sulphite may be added to the fresh must at this point, *must* be added if California grapes are used. The amateur who is

Fill containers three-fourths full.

not planning to use a yeast starter should be careful not to overdose, as too large a dose of "meta" inhibits fermenta-tion.[5] The mouths of the fermenting-containers are then wiped dry and plugged with bungs of absorbent cotton.

TESTING THE MUST

The must should be tested for sugar content as soon as pos-sible, with a saccharometer. The sugar content having been

[5] A safe dose is 7 gm. (¼ oz.) per 20 gallons. If a starter is to be used, a safe dose is 10 gm. (⅓ oz.) per 20 gallons. If the total vintage is divided among several bottles, dissolve the total dose in a small quantity of water and then distribute the solution evenly among the bottles. If fermentation does not start spontaneously in two or three days, aerate the juice by racking (i.e., siphoning, or by pouring from one container to another).

determined, adjustment should be made if necessary by the addition of the correct amount of cane sugar, according to the table on page 124. It is easier to adjust the sugar content for white wine than for red because the juice has already been separated from skins and pulp and its quantity is accurately known.

> EXAMPLE. *The saccharometer shows 17 degrees Balling or 9.2 Dujardin-Salleron. Reference to the sugar table on page 124 indicates an addition of 5.98 oz. per gallon to make a wine of 12 per cent alcohol by volume. Total quantity of sugar to add is 20 × 5.98 oz., which equals 119.6 oz. or 7.47 lb. This should be dissolved in a small quantity of the juice, or of warm water. If water is used, add enough extra sugar to compensate for the increased volume.*

At this point the test for total acidity should be made, if it is to be made.[6] If acidity is too high, it may be reduced by discreet dilution with a sugar-and-water solution adjusted to 20 degrees Balling (or 11.2 Dujardin). With high-acid Eastern varieties, such dilution may be carried to the point of one gallon to four gallons of fresh must.

As white wines are almost invariably deficient in tannin, it is a good rule to correct with 1 gram of pure dry tannic acid for every four gallons of must, dissolved in ¼ cupful of warm water, adding directly to the must, and stirring in. The tannin must be best-quality U.S.P. If the wine-maker has any doubts, he should not use the tannin.

One of the more controversial questions in the making of white wine has to do with the advisability of *clearing* the must before fermentation begins. This is usually done,

---

[6] See page 127.

when done at all, by allowing the fresh must to settle for twelve to twenty-four hours. This brings down the sediment (consisting of dust of vineyard soil carried into the must on the grapes, and other relatively insoluble matter), and the must is then racked (i.e., siphoned) from the sediment into clean containers before the fermentation gets underway. If the must is cool, the settling takes place spontaneously before fermentation begins; the addition of metabisulphite, by retarding or preventing the commencement of the fermentation, also aids settling.

The theory behind preliminary clarification of the must is that it promotes a cleaner fermentation and gets rid of much undesirable material at the very beginning of the process. The theory appeals to one's reason; and undoubtedly it holds true if the grapes have a low total acidity or are not in first-class condition at the time of crushing. At any rate, clearing is practiced a good deal in California and other hot winegrowing regions. But of recent years the practice has gone out of vogue in many enlightened wine-making areas, for the reason that clearing also eliminates certain substances, particularly the pectic constituents of the must, which contribute to the production of a superior wine—contribute "softness" especially. Thus the wisdom of the practice is very much open to doubt, and the amateur winemaker may safely skip it.

THE FERMENTATION

The containers are filled only three-fourths to four-fifths full of must in order to avoid the possibility of overflow when the fermentation begins, a fermentation which is never so violent, however, as that of red wine. If a yeast starter is to be used, it may be added eight to twelve hours after pressing. The wine-maker should if possible see that

The crown is formed.

the temperature of the fermenting-room is not too high. The usual practice is to ferment white wines at temperatures somewhat lower than red. If a yeast starter is used, evidence of fermentation should be visible in a matter of hours in the form of slowly rising bubbles. If spontaneous fermentation is being depended upon, evidence of it should appear within twenty-four to forty-eight hours. The first symptom is the appearance of clots of fine foam on the surface of the liquid,[7] and a rim of bubbles around the edge, followed by the gradual rising and diffusion of the sediment that has set-

[7] Sometimes there is a preliminary growth of what will look to the wine-maker like ordinary bread mold. This need not worry him.

tled at the bottom of the container. The clots of foam coalesce rapidly, and soon there develops a thick layer of bubbles. The French describe this by saying that *"le moût forme sa couronne* (the must is forming its crown)."* Sometimes the bubbles are small, sometimes enormous, like the soap bubbles children blow. Whether the bubbles are large or small depends on the viscosity of the must, and that varies, of course, according to the character of the grapes.

A gentle bubbling sound may also be heard at the mouth of the bottle.

When the fermentation is well started, the temperature should be held, if possible, at around 65° F. The danger of the development of bad ferments, which is more to be feared in the making of white wine than of red, is thus kept at a minimum.

If fermentation does not begin within twenty-four hours, either (a) the must is too cold, in which case the temperature should be raised or the must moved to a warmer spot, or (b) the dose of metabisulphite was a bit too strong, in which case the must should be siphoned or poured from one container to another (sediment and all) in order to aerate it and thus reduce the quantity of SO_2 present. As white wine has not the advantage of the great initial quantity of yeast which is on the skins, its fermentation ordinarily proceeds at a more deliberate pace than that of red wine. Although on occasion it may ferment very rapidly, more usually two to three weeks are required.

During fermentation the sugar content should be tested every few days in order to ascertain the progress of the fermentation.

At intervals the cotton stoppers should be examined. If they have become damp, they should be changed for fresh ones.

The end of violent fermentation is indicated by the gradual precipitation of the sediment, or lees, which is composed of the solid matter originally in the must and kept in suspension during fermentation, yeast that has died or ceased to be active, and certain other substances normally precipitated during the course of fermentation, chiefly cream of tartar. The end of the violent fermentation is also indicated by the saccharometer, which falls to *below* zero.

When the violent fermentation has been concluded, the vintage is consolidated, which is to say that the containers are filled full.

EXAMPLE. *If a vintage of 20 gallons was fermented in five five-gallon bottles each filled ⅘ full, the newly fermented wine in one of these bottles is used to fill the empty space in the other four.*

The new wine is *not* racked or siphoned from its sediment at this time (for reasons that will become clear in the next chapter), but is left to rest on its sediment. The important thing is that *all containers must be filled full when fermentation ceases.* Not to fill them full is to run the risk of spoiling the wine. When filled, the containers are again wiped clean and stoppers of fresh absorbent cotton inserted. The wine is then set aside for its secondary fermentation. Subsequent treatment of white wine is the same as that of red wine, and is the subject of the two following chapters.

IF BLACK GRAPES ARE USED

If the wine-maker has access only to black grapes but wishes to make white wine, he may do so provided his grapes are not one of the varieties known as *teinturiers*.[8] The grapes should be cool at the time of crushing and pressing, and ought not to be dead ripe. They should be crushed and pressed as swiftly as possible, and only the juice from the first gentle pressing should be used. Even though this juice may be faintly pink, the color will normally oxidize and disappear in the course of fermentation. After taking the first light pressing, the wine-maker may then place the partly pressed pomace in a vat and ferment it as he would for the production of red wine. This is called mixed fermentation. It is worth a try, if only to show how different two wines from the same grapes may be.

If in spite of all precautions the pressed juice contains considerable color, it may be fermented to produce what the French call *vin gris*, a sort of pale rosé which, lacking the elements contributed to red wine by the skins, will in spite of its color have more the quality of a white wine than of a red. Musts containing too much color to make a natural white wine may also be bleached by the addition of special decolorizing charcoals, but these are hard to handle and, if not of the best quality, may leave a disagreeable taste in the wine; their use is not recommended. Musts containing too much color for use as white wine may be blended, after fermentation, with red wine. Red wines so ameliorated gain in *finesse* but lose in body.

[8] The *teinturier* varieties have color in the juice as well as in the skins.

CHAPTER X

The Secondary Fermentation

After the wine has finished its primary or violent fermentation, a good deal more must happen before it is ready to be drunk. The next step in its evolution is what is called the secondary fermentation. Some knowledge of what takes place during this phase is necessary if the wine-maker is to handle his wine intelligently.

At the end of the violent fermentation the young wine still contains a residue of unfermented sugar. Until recently it had always been supposed that the secondary fermentation is merely a more leisurely extension of the primary, a sort of cleanup of this residue. But investigations during the past quarter-century have revealed some surprising facts about the secondary fermentation—facts that go far to explain certain mysterious changes which take place in many young wines. It has been found that the fermentation of the residual sugar shades off gradually into another and wholly different kind of fermentation—a bacterial fermentation which has nothing to do with sugar or alcohol *but is con-*

cerned solely with the acidity of the wine. This is called the malo-lactic fermentation.

It will be recalled [1] that musts contain two predominant organic acids in varying quantities: tartaric acid, which is the acid peculiarly associated with grape juice; and malic acid, an acid much more widely distributed in the plant world. The proportions of these two acids vary greatly. Generally speaking, the proportion of malic acid is high in unripe grapes and low in ripe grapes. What happens in malo-lactic fermentation is that certain strains of bacteria attack the malic (but not the tartaric) acid in the young wine and transform it into the much feebler lactic acid [2] plus a certain quantity of carbon dioxide gas. This transformation is most simply expressed in the following formula:

$$H_2C_4H_4O_5 \xrightarrow{\text{(lactic bacteria)}} HC_3H_5O_3 + CO_2$$

(malic acid) (lactic acid) (carbon dioxide)

What the malo-lactic fermentation does, then, when it replaces the malic with the lactic acid, is to *cause a sharp reduction in total acidity.*

Obviously, the effect of the malo-lactic fermentation is most pronounced in those regions where the grapes are most likely to contain a high proportion of malic acid, which is to say, where they ripen with the most difficulty— such regions as the Rhineland of Germany, the Burgundy district in France, and much of the Eastern United States. Its effect is least pronounced in regions where the grapes ripen with ease and indeed tend to be overripe by the time they are picked—such as the south of France, Italy, and

[1] See Chapter VI.
[2] An acid not originally present in grape juice. It is the acid of sour milk.

California. It is this hitherto unsuspected malo-lactic fermentation that takes the "hardness" or "greenness" out of a young Rhine wine or a Burgundy and ultimately produces a wine which is soft, pleasing, and well-balanced. It is this malo-lactic fermentation that also explains certain hitherto mysterious accidents which sometimes occur in wines after they have been bottled. For if a wine is bottled before the malo-lactic fermentation has run its course, there is always the danger that it will start up in the bottle itself. As carbon-dioxide gas is a byproduct and there is no way for it to escape from a corked bottle, the wine becomes turbid, gassy, and virtually undrinkable. This accident used to be especially troublesome in the Burgundy region.

HOW TO PROCEED

In presiding over the secondary fermentation the wine-maker, therefore, takes care to establish conditions that will encourage the malo-lactic bacteria to do their work promptly and thoroughly.

The storage space should be maintained if possible at a temperature range between 65° and 70° F. through the month of November, since the malo-lactic ferments work best within this range.

During this period the containers should not be bunged tight, since the small quantity of gas that is the byproduct of the fermentation must escape. The containers should either be equipped with fermentation valves (which let the gas out while not allowing the air to enter) or be plugged with absorbent cotton.

No SO_2 should be added to the new wine until after the

malo-lactic fermentation is completed, for the bacteria will not function in the presence of this antiseptic.

If the temperature of the storage space unavoidably drops before the malo-lactic fermentation is finished, its resump-

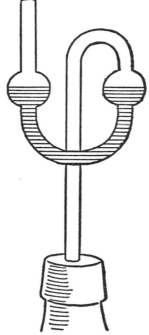

Fermentation valve.

tion should be looked for with the rise of temperature in the following spring.

During this period, if the wine is stored in cooperage, there will be considerable shrinkage. The containers should in that case be refilled, or "topped," at regular intervals. The best method is to settle on a certain day of the week, so that weekly topping becomes a matter of habit. The topping is done preferably with wine of the same type, but in any case with similar wine of good quality. *The importance of keeping the containers full cannot be exaggerated.*

Practically speaking, the end of the secondary fermentation is signified when the bubbles of carbon dioxide cease to be given off. From this point on, the wine may be more tightly bunged, topping may be done once every two weeks instead of once a week, and the temperature of the storage space may be allowed to drop.

The conclusion of the secondary fermentation can be determined more definitely (if the wine-maker wants to take the trouble) by a chemical test. Specific tests for tartaric, malic, and lactic acids are difficult. Fortunately they are not necessary. What the wine-maker can do is to test the young wine for *total acidity* periodically during secondary fermentation. If he notices a drop in total acidity, he infers that malo-lactic fermentation is under way. When total acidity ceases to drop, he may infer that it is finished. Successive comparative tests for total acidity are thus the sure indicator of the progress of the malo-lactic fermentation.

There exists one sort of situation in which the beneficial malo-lactic fermentation requires special encouragement: namely, when the total acidity of the wine is truly excessive. A total acidity of more than 1.1 per cent [3] discourages the necessary multiplication of the malo-lactic organisms themselves. In such a case it is necessary to reduce the total acidity *by chemical means* to a point at which the malo-lactic organisms can take hold and do their job. This is done by the addition of a small quantity of *pure precipitated chalk* (drugstore grade), which neutralizes an equivalent quantity of the acid present in the wine.

---

[3] That is 11 grams per liter as tartaric.

But this reduction of acidity by chemical means must be undertaken with great circumspection, because the chalk acts in a very special way. What it does is to combine by preference with the *tartaric* acid present rather than with the malic, and this (if too much is added) brings about an abnormal situation in which virtually all of the acidity of the wine consists of *malic*. Then, when the malo-lactic organisms undertake and carry through their work of eliminating the malic, the wine, far from having too much total acidity, has too little. In this sort of chemical deacidification, then, the object is to eliminate a part only, *not all*, of the tartaric acid present—just enough to provide favorable conditions for the onset of the malo-lactic fermentation. If one must deacidify, a safe rule is never to risk a dose of chalk larger than one gram per liter of wine.

The two following examples illustrating the effect of malo-lactic fermentation were kindly supplied to me by A. de Chaunac, of Bright's Wines, Ltd., from his records. In example No. 1, an experimental vintage of white wine, malo-lactic fermentation proceeded normally. In example No. 2, a vintage of red wine, variety Landot 244, the malo-lactic fermentation had to be started with chalk.

EXAMPLE NO. 1. RAVAT 6, 1951 VINTAGE

PERCENTAGE OF TOTAL ACIDITY

Oct. 5. Pressed juice for fermenting	1.03
Oct. 23. Wine	1.05
Nov. 12. Wine	.90
Dec. 16. Wine	.81
Dec. 16. Wine (chilled)	.69

Wine fermented in a 50-gallon barrel, then on Oct. 23 racked to a 25-gallon barrel and surplus kept for ullage.

Dec. 31 wine racked to carboys. Jan. 10 finings added. Jan. 28 wine filtered and bottled, final total acidity .68%. Alcohol 12.3%.

EXAMPLE NO. 2. LANDOT 244, 1951 VINTAGE

	PERCENTAGE OF TOTAL ACIDITY
Sept. 24. Crushed grapes for fermenting	1.36
Sept. 28. Pressed, put in carboys	1.18
Nov. 12. Wine	1.18

As no malo-lactic fermentation was under way, added 1 gm. per liter of chalk, bringing total acidity to 1.03/1.00.

	PERCENTAGE OF TOTAL ACIDITY [*]
Dec. 4. Fermenting	.92 to .98
Dec. 12. Fermenting	.72 to .96
Dec. 20. Racked and mixed, as one carboy was not fermenting as fast as others.	
Jan. 21. To cold room, 25° F.	
Feb. 4. Filtered and bottled. Total acidity, .72%. Alcohol, 11.0%.	

[*] In different carboys.

It is now necessary to mention an important exception to the instructions given in the paragraphs above. When a wine-maker is working with dead-ripe grapes, as in California, he is not concerned about the reduction of excessive acidity: he is concerned instead about insufficient acidity. Thus the interest of wine-makers using California grapes is to preserve a maximum total acidity in his wine, *whether the acid be tartaric or malic*. It is to his interest, in other words, to make sure that the malo-lactic fermentation *does not* take place—and, furthermore, *will not* take place after the wine is in bottle. This he does by adding a moderate dose of metabisulphite (2 gm. per 20 gallons) to the new wine as soon as in his judgment the fermentation of residual sugar has been finished, and by racking the new wine from its lees as soon as the wine has cleared itself of its sediment, by December 1 at the latest. From then on, the malo-lactic fermentation is inhibited and the stability of the new wine is assured by the addition of the same moderate dose of SO_2 (2 gm. of metabisulphite per 20 gallons) at each subsequent racking.

CHAPTER XI

Finishing the Wine

Somewhere between the end of November and mid-December the wine begins to lose its roughness, yeastiness, and turbidity and may, indeed, be quite clear and even fairly agreeable to taste. This is the time for a checkup of the wine's composition. Very few amateurs bother with a real chemical analysis, yet they are better off if at least they know the tests involved and understand the purpose of them. The usual analyses are for *alcoholic content, total acidity,* and *volatile acidity.*[1]

TESTING FOR ALCOHOLIC CONTENT

The wine-maker knows in advance what the approximate alcoholic content of his wine is going to be; but there are occasions when it may be desirable to check the predicted alcoholic content against an actual test. The method of

---

[1] Commercial wineries also analyze at this point or subsequently for free and combined SO_2 and for "dry extract," or non-sugar solids.

analysis here given is known as the distillation [2] method.

Equipment.[3] One 300 cc. *Pyrex flask* and *glass condenser* or *"worm"* with its support; one 100 cc. *graduated beaker;*

Small distillation apparatus, or "alambic," for testing alcoholic content.

one *hydrometer for light liquids;* one *hydrometer jar.*

Procedure. Measure 100 cc. of the wine in the beaker and place it in the flask. Measure 50 cc. of water and add that to

[2] Most wineries, while reserving the distillation method for occasions when great precision is necessary, use an instrument called an *ebulliometer*, which is based on the principle that an alcohol solution has a lower boiling-point than water. This is quick and simple, but an ebulliometer is expensive.

[3] This equipment may be bought from a dealer in laboratory equipment. The French firm of Dujardin-Salleron manufactures a small and quite inexpensive boxed alcohol-testing kit, which provides the equivalent of the equipment here described.

SPECIFIC-GRAVITY TABLE

(*The correspondence between specific gravity and alcoholic content of mixtures of alcohol and water at 60° F.*)

SP. GR. AT 60° F.	PER CENT BY VOL.	PER CENT BY WT.	SP. GR. AT 60° F.	PER CENT BY VOL.	PER CENT BY WT.
1.00000	0.0	0.00	0.98374	12.5	10.09
0.99925	0.5	0.40	0.98319	13.0	10.50
0.99850	1.0	0.80	0.98264	13.5	10.91
0.99776	1.5	1.19	0.98210	14.0	11.32
0.99703	2.0	1.59	0.98157	14.5	11.73
0.99630	2.5	1.99	0.98104	15.0	12.14
0.99559	3.0	2.39	0.98051	15.5	12.55
0.99488	3.5	2.79	0.97998	16.0	12.96
0.99419	4.0	3.19	0.97946	16.5	13.37
0.99350	4.5	3.60	0.97895	17.0	13.79
0.99282	5.0	4.00	0.97844	17.5	14.20
0.99215	5.5	4.40	0.97794	18.0	14.61
0.99150	6.0	4.80	0.97744	18.5	15.03
0.99085	6.5	5.21	0.97694	19.0	15.44
0.99022	7.0	5.61	0.97645	19.5	15.85
0.98960	7.5	6.02	0.97596	20.0	16.27
0.98899	8.0	6.42	0.97546	20.5	16.68
0.98838	8.5	6.83	0.97496	21.0	17.10
0.98779	9.0	7.23	0.97446	21.5	17.52
0.98720	9.5	7.64	0.97395	22.0	17.93
0.98661	10.0	8.05	0.97344	22.5	18.35
0.98602	10.5	8.45	0.97293	23.0	18.77
0.98544	11.0	8.86	0.97241	23.5	19.19
0.98487	11.5	9.27	0.97189	24.0	19.60
0.98430	12.0	9.68	0.97137	24.5	20.02
			0.97084	25.0	20.44

EXAMPLE. *Suppose the specific-gravity reading is 0.98430. According to the table, a specific gravity of 0.98430 indicates an alcoholic content of 9.68 per cent by weight or 12 per cent by volume. (Alcoholic content is usually stated* by volume.)

the wine in the flask. Attach the condenser to the flask and fill the cooling-space of the condenser with cold water. Rinse the beaker and place it at the lower end of the condenser. Heat the flask gently over a gas or alcohol burner. Vapor will begin to pass into the coil, where it will be condensed and drop gradually into the beaker. The condensing bath should be replaced occasionally with more cold water. Collect *almost* 100 cc. of the condensate, and to that add enough water to bring it to exactly 100 cc. This is exactly the volume of the wine originally placed in the flask; but it consists only of the alcohol of the wine plus water, with all other substances eliminated. Cool the condensate to about 60° F. and pour it into the hydrometer jar. Insert the hydrometer and take the reading. The percentage of alcohol by weight or volume is determined from this reading by reference to the Specific-Gravity Table.

TESTING FOR ACIDITY

The acidity of wine is furnished partly by the *fixed acids* (which are tartaric, malic, and lactic) and partly by *volatile acids*, which are products of fermentation and are present in much smaller quantity provided the wine is sound.

The fixed acids, as we know, are considerably reduced, during primary and secondary fermentation, partly by malo-lactic fermentation and partly by precipitation of cream of tartar.

The volatile acids to be found in new wine are carbonic acid (which gradually escapes as carbon-dioxide gas), acetic acid, butyric acid, and propionic acid. A small quantity of these is found in all wine, and in small quantity they serve an important role in the development of the *bouquet*. Bouquet is never present in new wine and develops only with aging; chemically it consists of *ethers* which are formed by the action of the volatile acids on the higher alcohols contained in the wine. If there were no volatile acids at all, no true bouquet would develop.

But the presence of volatile acids in more than a very small quantity is invariably a sign of disease. Volatile acid, as Bernard says, is "the pulse which tells at any moment the state of health of the wine." The allowable maximum under California regulations is 1.1 gm. per liter, expressed as acetic acid.

In testing for volatile acidity, the first step is to determine the *total acidity* by the same test that was used in determining the total acidity of the must before fermentation (see page 127). If the total acidity of the new wine is lower than was the total acidity of the must, and has a clean, vinous smell, then the wine-maker may infer that his wine is sound and he need not bother to determine what proportion of the total consists of fixed acids and what proportion consists of volatile acids.

DETERMINING VOLATILE ACIDITY

If, however, the new wine shows a total acidity higher than that of the must from which it was made, it is important to go farther and determine whether the volatile acidity exceeds the safe minimum. In doing this, the first step is to use one's nose. The undesirable volatile acids all have highly pungent and characteristic odors. Acetic acid, which is the one most to be feared, has the odor of vinegar. Propionic acid has an odor resembling that of acetic acid. Butyric acid smells like rancid butter (it is, indeed, the same substance that gives rancid butter its smell). Thus, if the volatile acids increase much beyond the danger point, they have a way of announcing themselves.

There is also a means of determining chemically the volatile-acid content (the method devised by W. V. Cruess and R. W. Bettoli) which is not too difficult. By this method the volatile acidity is determined indirectly. That is, the total acidity and the fixed acidity are determined, and the volatile acidity is then determined by subtracting one from the other.

Procedure. First decolorize 75 cc. of the wine by allowing it to stand with bone-black that is free from carbonates. Impure bone-black containing carbonates cannot be used. Bone-black absorbs the coloring matter. The decolorized wine is filtered and should be water-white. Titrate 20 cc. of this wine with .1 normal sodium hydroxide (NaOH). Record the cc. of NaOH used from titrating and call this "A." Then take 20 cc. more of the decolorized sample and mix with approximately 2 grams of common salt (NaCl) in a 200-cc. Erlenmeyer flask. Boil down this liquid rapidly on a gas or alcohol flame until a copious separation of NaCl takes place and the wine begins to spatter. Then pour into the flask 20 cc. of distilled water and boil down until the NaCl separates again. Dilute this remaining liquid again with distilled water to a volume of 20 cc. and titrate with .1 normal NaOH. Record the cc. used for titration and call this "B." Then:

(A — B) × .3 = volatile acid grams per liter
expressed as acetic.

The factor .3 is explained as follows: 1 cc. of .1 normal
NaOH = .006 grams acetic acid. Using a 60-cc. sample,
the factor would be .1 because $\dfrac{\text{cc. NaOH} \times .006}{60} \times 1,000$
becomes cc. NaOH × .1 in calculating the grams of acetic
acid per 1,000 cc. (liter) of wine. As our sample is one third
of 60, or 20 cc., the factor is three times as large, or .3.

Equipment needed: burner, Erlenmeyer flasks, 20-cc.
pipettes, 3-inch glass funnel, filter paper, burette graduated
in .1 cc.; supply of .1 NaOH, pure bone-black, indicator
(either litmus or phenolphthalein solution).

INTERPRETING THE TESTS

Assuming that the wine-maker has made these tests, what
do they mean? To what use will the results be put?

Alcohol. If the wine has been properly made, alcoholic
content will be found to fall between 11 and 13 per cent
by volume, in which case the test for alcoholic content
merely confirms that things are as they should be. If alcoholic content is deficient, the wise thing to do is to *blend
with a wine of higher alcoholic content.*

Acidity. Wine that shows a high *volatile* acidity (over
1.1 gm. per liter as acetic) is in bad shape. The thing to do
is to stop all further development of the volatile acidity and
finish and consume the wine as rapidly as possible. The wine
is racked immediately from its lees, or sediment, and a dose

of potassium metabisulphite [4] is added during the racking. The wine is then chilled, fined, bottled, and used immediately thereafter without bottle-aging.

If the volatile acidity is already so high as to be disagreeably noticeable on smelling the wine, the best thing to do is to dump the wine and forget it, as a badly diseased wine can never be brought back to a condition of health. Never try to rescue a bad wine by blending it with a good. The result is merely to spoil the good wine.

If the wine has a high total acidity—if the wine, that is, is simply too tart but is otherwise sound-smelling and of good constitution—the chances are that the malo-lactic fermentation has not run its course. In this case, several choices are open to the wine-maker: (1) he may continue to keep his wine in a moderately warm place, trusting to nature to initiate and complete the malo-lactic chore; (2) he may reduce the acidity slightly by chemical means in order to encourage the malo-lactic ferments; [5] (3) he may achieve the same effect by blending with a low-acid wine. Of the three methods, the third is the conservative one and, generally speaking, the best.

If the wine shows a low total acidity—if the wine, that is, tastes flat and insipid though otherwise sound—then the obvious thing to do is to blend with a high-acid wine. It is also possible to improve such wines by the discreet addition of pure tartaric acid, obtainable at the drugstore in

[4] The correct dose is 1 gm. per 5 gallons, or 10 gm. per 50-gallon barrel, dissolved in a small quantity of warm water and mixed into the wine as it is being racked.

[5] By adding 1 gm. per liter of pure precipitated chalk. See Example No. 2, p. 154.

powdered form. This is done frequently in the California wineries, but should always be done sparingly and never to the extent of more than 1 gm. tartaric acid per liter.

Blending. This has been mentioned several times in the paragraphs above. In blending, a few elementary rules should be observed:

1. Make a small blend first, in a graduated glass. Then make the large blend proportionately.

2. The wines entering into a blend should all be absolutely sound. The outcome of a blend of a sound wine with an unsound wine can only be disastrous.

3. Wines from Eastern-grown grapes, which as a rule are rather low in alcohol and high in acidity, will blend well with wines from California grapes, with their opposite characteristics.

4. The wines to be blended should be if possible of approximately the same age.

5. Never blend a sweet wine with a dry wine.

RACKING

By the time the secondary fermentation has run its course, the wine will have gone a long way toward clearing itself, the greater part of the suspended matter that made it so muddy in the beginning having settled to the bottom of the container. When the wine-maker has completed his tests for alcoholic content and acidity (or decided to forgo them), it is time for the first racking. This is nothing more than the separation of the wine from the sediment, or lees, by siphoning, by draining through a bunghole, or by pumping. The lees consist of yeast cells, most of the other organisms previously present in the new wine, cream of tartar, albuminous matter, and various other substances that the wine must throw off before it becomes really bright and clear and drinkable. Racking is, then, a partial purification. Repeated often enough, and carefully enough, racking is almost as effective as sterilization. Another reason for racking is that though a wine may become perfectly clear while resting on its lees, a renewed fermentation brought on by warm weather lifts the lees into suspension again, causing the wine to become turbid. This cannot happen if the lees have already been eliminated. The oxidative effect of racking often helps to clarify the wine by promoting the precipitation of certain constituents; but this oxidation can also be dangerous. In light white wines especially, it may cause a darkening of color, accompanied by the development of a not very agreeable Madeira-like, or sherry-like, taste. This effect is called "maderization" by the wine-makers, and will be returned to farther on.

When to Rack. For red wines, it is well to give the first racking in mid-December, after the conclusion of the secondary fermentation.[6] It is racked a second time in February, before the coming of warm weather. The wine is ordinarily racked a third time in June. If it is a wine likely to profit by further racking, it is racked a fourth time in October, in order to rid it of any lees that have been thrown down during the hot weather. If held longer before bottling, it is racked once or twice a year. Between rackings,

---

[6] But in California, where the malo-lactic fermentation is not desired, this first racking takes place sooner—just as soon as the wine has begun to clear.

the containers must, of course, be "topped" regularly to prevent an air space. Racking is preferably done in bright, clear weather, such as often coincides with a full moon. The choice of such a time is not superstition. Clear weather usually means high atmospheric pressure, and when atmospheric pressure is high, the light lees are less likely to be disturbed and drawn over in the course of racking.

White wine, like red, is normally racked four times during the first year of its life. There is a trend, however, toward early bottling of light white wines, for the sake of preserving their freshness and fruitiness. For most white wines, it is advantageous to bottle after two rackings; and in certain white-wine regions it is customary not to rack at all. The wine is allowed to clear naturally on its original lees and is bottled directly from the lees before the advent of warm weather in the spring.[7] This is the settled practice in Switzerland and Austria and is quite frequent in Germany and Alsace. It is a practice that might well be more generally adopted for light white wines produced in the Eastern United States.

The First Racking.[8] Racking is not an onerous task; on the contrary, as befits a rite of purification, it is a cheerful occasion, to be followed if possible by drinking and feasting. But the prospect of the feast should never be allowed to interfere with the proper performance of the rite. The siphoning hose may be sterilized by soaking in water heated to just below the boiling-point, and the container that is to receive the racked wine must be thoroughly rinsed. This

[7] This cannot be done, of course, unless the wine falls perfectly clear and bright.
[8] I assume that the wine to be racked has undergone its secondary fermentation in five-gallon bottles.

container naturally has to be placed lower than that from which the wine is being racked; hence the desirability of benches or shelves. If the wine container is lifted before the racking, it should be lifted very gently in order not to disturb the lees.

When the containers are in place for racking, remove the water valve or plug of cotton from one of them. Insert the notched end of the siphon tube into the wine—not too far down, for that will disturb the lees. Start the flow by the traditional method of sucking, and let the wine flow into the clean container. The wine as it is racked should be allowed to flow from the tube down along the inside of the clean container; this aerates the new wine thoroughly, and such aeration is good for it at this first racking, though not subsequently.

When one of the containers has been emptied, rinse it, and it is then ready to receive the racked wine from the next container.

When the first racking has been concluded and the new containers are *full*, cork them well, but not too firmly.[9] The storage place should no longer be warm. The wine profits at this stage by a prolonged and thorough chilling, which promotes clarification and further softens the wine by precipitation of more cream of tartar.

Later Rackings. Procedure for later rackings is identical with that of the first, with two exceptions. The wine should not be aerated, but should be kept out of contact with the air as much as possible. This is done by plunging the outlet end of the siphon tube *below* the surface of the liquid in

[9] For such small vintages in glass, wrap the cork in ordinary kitchen paraffin paper.

Racking and aerating new wine.

the container that is being filled. Thus only the surface is exposed, and the chance of overoxidation is reduced. During these later rackings the wine should be lightly sulphured.[1] This SO_2, thus dispersed in the wine, has a mild

---

[1] By adding, for each 5-gallon bottle, a pinch (0.5 gm.) of metabisulphite dissolved in an ounce or so of warm water and poured into the bottle just as racking begins.

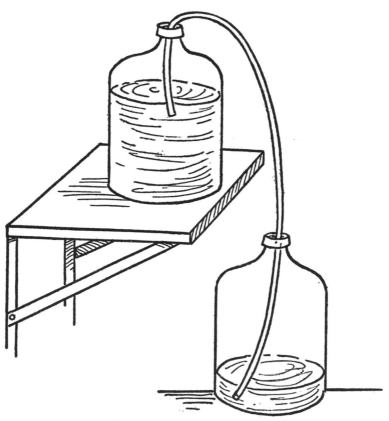

Racking new wine without aeration.

antiseptic and antioxidizing effect, which protects the wine against accident and in no way harms it.

In the course of the first racking it is hardly possible to avoid bringing over some little of the lees with the wine. But little or no lees come over with subsequent rackings, if they are carefully done.

169

FINING

Fining is the art of helping the wine, by the addition of various substances (called *finings*), to precipitate every last trace of suspended matter and thus to become perfectly clear and brilliant. A healthy wine will usually clear itself, soon or late. But often a wine that is well-balanced and healthy fails to clear itself promptly or completely. This is more likely to be true of a young white wine than of a young red wine, owing to the normal deficiency of tannin in white wine. Such wines should always be fined. The test for brilliance is simply to hold a lighted match or candle, in a dark room, behind a glass or a five-gallon bottle of the wine: the outline of the flame should be clear and sharp. If the flame is fuzzy, the wine should be fined.

A number of rather different materials are used for fining; and these fall into two categories: mineral finings and organic finings.

The mineral finings are clays, traditionally kaolin, or Spanish clay. In the United States the usual mineral fining material is bentonite, a closely related material available to wine-makers in a refined form. The organic finings are gelatin, isinglass (fish glue), white of egg, and casein in various compounds, including skim milk.

Bentonite is the most commonly used fining material in the bulk wine industry, as its use is simple and easy. But it is rarely used for superior wines, and the amateur has nothing to gain from it.

Of the organic finings, gelatin is far and away the most popular. What gelatin does is to form a coarse flocculation by combination with some of the tannin present in the wine. The wine's suspended matter is entrained by the flocculating material and drawn to the bottom as the finings gradually settle. Since red wine is rich in tannin, the fining of red wine consists simply in adding, and stirring in, the proper quantity of gelatin,[2] which has been previously dissolved in a small quantity of warm water. The amateur wine-maker cannot do better than buy ordinary household gelatin at his grocery store, but he should be sure that he gets the unflavored. With the use of gelatin, the wine normally falls bright in from four to fifteen days. Gelatin fining is most effective on cold wine.

As white wine is normally deficient in tannin, it should be prepared for fining by the previous addition of a dose of pure dissolved tannin, so that the gelatin, added afterwards, will have something to combine with. *Tannin should be added in a dose equal in weight to the gelatin dose to be added.*

The one serious danger in the use of gelatin is that called *overfining*, which is simply the addition of a dose of gelatin larger than is necessary for the purpose. In an overfined wine, what happens is that the excess gelatin [3] stays permanently in suspension, giving rise to a persistent cloudiness, which is extremely difficult to deal with. Overfining occurs with white wine, never with red. The cure for overfining is

[2] *Dose:* The safe dose for the small-scale wine-maker is 2 gm. per 5 gallons of wine. Household gelatin comes ready-measured in ¼-oz. (7-gm.) envelopes. A photographer's scale is useful for measuring small doses.

[3] Beyond that which has tannin to combine with.

to chill the wine, rack it in the presence of air, and then add a dose of dissolved tannin equal to one half of the original dose.

Isinglass yields an even more brilliant clarification than gelatin, but its use is difficult and will not be described here. To use white of egg, beat it lightly in advance with a small quantity of water, add it to the wine, and stir. No tannin is needed. The white of an egg of average size has a fining power equivalent to a gelatin dose of three to four grams. The caseins are no longer in fashion, as they do not yield a brilliant clarification under normal conditions. They have one important advantage, however: namely, a certain decolorizing power. This makes them useful occasionally in the fining of white wines that are a little too dark in color. The casein salts normally used are potassium caseinate and sodium caseinate, and of these the first is preferable. They are added at the rate of 4 ounces per 100 gallons (6 gm. per 5-gallon bottle). The caseins are flocculated by the acidity of the wine and not, as is gelatin, by the tannin. One of the principal difficulties in using casein is that flocculation is almost instantaneous, so that it takes the form of large curds that are not well dispersed throughout the wine. This difficulty may be overcome by injecting the casein solution (prepared in advance by dissolving in a small quantity of water) into the wine by means of a syringe.

Whichever fining material is used, the fining should be undertaken after the wine has achieved approximate stability, but without any great delay. This usually means from mid-January to the first of March. When the finings have fallen and the wine is bright, rack it. Long contact with the finings sometimes causes trouble.

FILTRATION

Although fining is the traditional method of clarifying wine that does not clear by settling alone, there are other ways of doing it, of which filtration is the principal one. Filtration is in a sense the reverse of fining. That is to say, when wine is fined, a sort of veil of the fining material is drawn down through the wine, dragging all suspended matter with it, whereas in filtration the veil, a porous wall or membrane, is fixed and the wine is forced through it, leaving the suspended material behind and emerging clear and bright. Filtration has had a long, hard struggle to establish itself in wineries. Early filtration methods were defective in two principal ways: First, the material through which the wine was filtered frequently imparted an off flavor or odor to the wine, and there was often metal pickup, caused by the fact that filters were often constructed of inappropriate metals. Second, wine frequently came into excessive contact with air, owing to faulty filter construction, and suffered the effects of overoxidation. These original difficulties, however, have been solved. Filtration is now practically universal in commercial wine-making.

The advantages are obvious. It clarifies the wine immediately, whereas fining takes time. It yields consistent results. It eliminates only the insoluble matter in the wine and involves no chemical reaction whatever with the wine itself. Finally, filtration may be undertaken at any point in the life of the wine, even while it is still in the course of fermentation, should that prove desirable. But suitable filters are expensive, even in the smallest sizes; and a poor filter is far worse than none at all. The amateur may content himself with the reflection that good wines were being made centuries before filters were even heard of.

BOTTLING

Bottling is a pleasant task. The wine has been brought safely through the crisis of birth and the dangers of its youth, and the principal hazards to which wines are exposed are left behind as the corks are driven home. The precise moment to bottle depends partly on the whim of the wine-maker, partly on the time at his disposal, and also on the character of the wine. But certain fundamental conditions must first be met if the operation of bottling is to be successful. *First*, the wine should be brilliantly clear before it goes into bottle. If not, the wine either will remain persistently cloudy or will form more sediment in bottle than a good wine should. *Second*, the aroma should be perfectly clean—free, for example, from any traces of the hydrogen-sulphide, or rotten-egg, odor.[4] *Third*, the wine should have been through a chilling-period, especially white wine, in order to make sure that all excess cream of tartar has been eliminated. Otherwise a precipitate of cream of tartar, known as *gravel* to wine-men, is liable to develop subsequently in bottle; and the wine is also liable to cloud up on being chilled. *Fourth*, the secondary fermentation should have been completed.

[4] An odor that sometimes develops slightly in wine during its youth, but may be eliminated, if it persists, by a racking in the presence of air.

These are the essential conditions. The time for bottling also varies depending on whether the wine is white or red. Most *white wines* benefit by a relatively early bottling, since prolonged aging, with its inevitable exposure of the wine to oxygen, tends to darken it, sometimes to give it a woody taste, and to destroy that freshness which should be one of its charms. It is a sound general rule to bottle white wine as soon as the wine-maker is assured of its stability, meaning from April through June. Certain "big" white wines, however, such as the white Burgundies and the white Bordeaux wines, are not bottled until they have gone through one summer. It is interesting to bottle part of a vintage early and the rest after a year of aging, and note the frequently marked difference in character.

Red wines are rarely bottled as early as white wines, though in some regions a certain amount of red wine is bottled very young as a specialty. Such, for example, are the *rouges printaniers* of Switzerland. But it is a good general rule not to bottle red wines until they are at least one year old. The four rackings that a red wine is normally given during its first year are highly beneficial to its quality, the oxidation so provided helping to eliminate its "new" taste and aroma, and to assure the stability of its color. When red wine is made in sufficient quantity, aging in good oak cooperage does undoubtedly contribute subtly to the development of the bouquet and flavor. Some "big" red wines gain in softness and palatability by a storage period much longer than one year, but they are few.

This is as good a point as any to discuss the question of bottle age, about which there exist many misconceptions. It is commonly supposed among those who don't drink wine that great age is in itself a desirable characteristic of wine. This is not necessarily true. On the other hand, it is wrong to suppose that nothing happens once wine goes into a bottle and is sealed there. When wine is bottled, a considerable quantity of oxygen goes into the bottle along with the wine. The first effect of this oxidation is disconcerting. A bottle of wine opened twenty-four hours after it has been bottled usually tastes flat. This is what wine-makers call "bottle sickness." It is a passing phase, however. There then ensues a reverse process, subtle in its nature and extremely complicated, whereby the natural fruitiness of the wine is gradually lost, bouquet begins to develop (in wine capable of developing a bouquet), and the wine undergoes a general softening and refinement. In all but a few types of white wines, this process is relatively slight; the wine reaches its maximum of quality in a matter of months, maintains this quality for a varying period of time (several years, ordinarily), and then begins a process of decline. In red wines, the effects of bottle-aging are much more marked. Even a relatively ordinary red wine undergoes a sensational improvement if allowed to age in bottle for two, three, or even ten years. This is true even more conspicuously of the great clarets and Burgundies. Most red wines, however, may be said to have reached their maximum of quality after a year or two in bottle, and there is no point in keeping them any longer. In the case of red wines of great age, as of white, the marvel is usually that they are drinkable at all.

Equipment for Bottling. Bottling requires wine bottles, wine corks, a bottle-filler, and a corker.

Bottles. Always use wine bottles, if possible, with the

correct traditional shapes. This may seem a small point, but wine does seem to taste better when poured from a wine

Classic wine bottle shapes (l. to r.) Burgundy, Claret and Sauternes, Rhine Wine.

bottle than when poured from a pop bottle. The traditional shapes are illustrated: dark-green claret bottles for red wine, light-green Burgundy bottles for either red wine or dry white wine, Sauternes bottles, either white or very pale green, for white wines, and Rhine wine bottles. The latter are to be had in brown or green, the German Moselles being traditionally bottled in green and the German Rhine wines in brown.[5] Wine bottles may be bought either new

[5] Many a "connoisseur" has dazzled others at the table by distinguishing a Moselle from a Rhine wine merely by noting the color of the bottles; but today green is also used for many Rhines.

or rewashed from bottle-supply houses. Let the classified index in the telephone directory be your guide. Second-hand rewashed bottles are just as good as new and considerably cheaper. Small-scale wine-makers who make an appropriate connection with a club or restaurant soon collect an ample supply.

Corks. The corks should be first-quality No. 9, 1½- or 1¾-inch straight wine corks. A bad cork is always a source of trouble. For wines that are not to be kept any great length of time in bottle, second-quality No. 8, 1¼-inch corks are satisfactory, and much cheaper. Corks may be re-used after rinsing and then boiling briefly—provided they have not been punctured all the way through with a corkscrew.

Bottle-Filler. Small lots of wine may be bottled with the same rubber siphon hose that is used in racking. There exist small stop-start devices that fit into the filling end of the tube and make accurate filling easier.

Corker. Several are illustrated. See pages 114 and 115.

Procedure. The first consideration is the condition of the wine. If this is satisfactory, rack the wine with great care so as to pick up no lees. During this final racking or filtration, a small dose of metabisulphite should be added, to counteract overoxidation and provide insurance against misbehavior of the wine after it is bottled. The dose for home-size vintages is very small—about 2 grams per 20 gallons of wine, or a pinch per 5-gallon bottle.

The wine being ready, prepare the bottles. If new, they should be rinsed with hot water and set upside down in a rack to drain. If previously used and not cleaned commercially, they should be soaked in a tub for several hours in a solution of washing soda, washed with a bottle brush, rinsed thoroughly, and set to drain. A small contraption that is attached to the water faucet and directs a stream of water into the bottle when the bottle is pressed down upon it speeds the rinsing tremendously.

Corks must be given preliminary preparation, to soften and clean them. Put them in a kettle, add water, and bring the water just to a boil. Soaking in water from 140° to 160° F. for twenty minutes will soften them sufficiently and sterilize them. The discolored water should then be drained off, and the corks should be given several additional rinsings in warm water. Just before being used, they should be drained. If too soft, they will not drive evenly. If too hard, they will give trouble. Experience will demonstrate this.

When the bottles are drained, line them up conveniently on the floor or a table and fill just into the neck. All of the wine in a container should be bottled at one time. Otherwise a large air space is left, and that is not good for the wine. Corking should follow immediately. In corking wine, a small air space (about ⅓ inch) is best left in the neck, as wine is usually quite cool when bottled and this air space allows for the expansion of the wine should it be stored in a warmer place. After corking, the bottles should be left standing upright for twenty-four hours to allow the air pressure in the neck of the bottle to equalize with outside air pressure, and to let the corks harden. As a precaution against deterioration of the corks, they may be sealed. There exist special lead foil and plastic caps for this purpose. For a small batch of wine, the traditional wax seal provides a pleasant finish. Mix one part of beeswax to four parts of rosin, melt these together in a tin can, and dip the mouth of the bottle into the mixture. Color the sealing wax to suit your fancy.[6] Some even imprint the top with a seal of their own devising while the wax is hardening—a pretty touch.

With bottling, the task of wine-making is finished. The bottles should be binned on their sides, so that the interior face of the cork, or crown, is kept constantly moist and the air bubble is in the middle of the bottle. The storage place should have an even temperature.

[6] Artists' tube pigments may be used for this purpose, being stirred in when the sealing wax is melted.

CHAPTER XII

Sick Wines and False Wines

It would be pleasant to be able to approach the question of sick wines with a brisk and cheerful bedside manner, bringing assurance that there is nothing to worry about. Unfortunately, a wine that shows symptoms of illness is usually so far gone that it is not worth rescuing. One cannot emphasize too strongly that the way to be sure of good wine is to give it a sound and vigorous fermentation in the beginning and to preserve it from infection ever after.

Still, wines do develop ailments from time to time, and it is well for the wine-maker to be able to recognize these and so guard against them in subsequent vintages. These ailments may be divided into three general categories: (1) biological illnesses, (2) chemical illnesses, and (3) accidents.

The principal biological diseases are acetic fermentation, flowers of wine, and diseases caused by anaerobic bacteria.

Acetic Fermentation. The presence of acetic fermentation is quickly evident, for its end product is the odor and flavor of vinegar. This fermentation is caused by several bacteria which attack the alcohol of the wine, *in the presence of air,* and convert the alcohol into acetic acid and water. If the process continues long enough, all the alcohol is used up. A controlled fermentation of this type is in fact the process by which vinegar is made commercially. The reaction is as follows:

$$C_2H_6O \;+\; O_2 \;=\; C_2H_4O_2 \;+\; H_2O$$

(alcohol) (oxygen) (acetic acid) (water)

Note that acetic fermentation can take place only in the presence of air—*which is to say, in wine containers that are not filled full.* Its onset is indicated not only by the odor but by a growth on the surface of the wine of a film, which consists of the acetic-acid and other so-called aerobic organisms. Since the acetic bacteria *must* have air, the obvious way to hold them at bay is to keep the container filled full. That is one of the reasons for making the "topping" of new wine a routine procedure. As for cures, none are truly effective. If a batch of wine should turn acetic, the best thing to do is to let the infection run its course and wind up with a supply of good wine vinegar.

Flowers of Wine. This disease is caused by a mold called *Mycoderma vini,* which is related to the yeasts. Like the vinegar bacteria, it develops only in the presence of air; but it is not nearly so destructive. Every wine-maker is familiar with the appearance of the so-called flowers [1] because of their tendency to develop a film on the surface of the wine —even the tiny surface in the neck of a five-gallon bottle of wine.

The flowers work by attacking the alcohol and convert-

[1] Called *flor* in Spain, *fleur* in France, and *flora* by Cato the Elder.

ing it into water and carbon dioxide (plus aromatic by-products), according to the following formula:

$$C_2H_6O \ + \ O_2 \ = \ 3H_2O \ + \ 2CO_2$$
$$\text{(alcohol)} \quad \text{(oxygen)} \quad \text{(water)} \quad \text{(carbon dioxide)}$$

If allowed to continue their work, the flowers, like the acetic bacteria, eventually eat up all the alcohol in the wine. The growth of flowers is of course prevented, or held down to a harmless minimum, by keeping containers full.

It should be added that in some circumstances the development of flowers is actually encouraged. The characteristic aroma of Spanish sherry, for example, is a byproduct of their development. But when this aroma occurs in ordinary dry white wines it is undesirable, as indeed is the accompanying darkening of color.

Anaerobic Bacteria. Agents of the two diseases previously mentioned are *aerobic;* that is, they develop only in the presence of air and may be kept under control by keeping the wine containers filled. Of several other diseases the active agents are certain *anaerobic* bacteria—organisms, that is to say, which do not require the presence of air for their existence and development. For this reason they are peculiarly insidious.

In the chapters dealing with fermentation, considerable emphasis was placed on the importance of keeping the temperature within certain defined limits, on the importance of adequate acidity in the must, and on the importance of protecting musts of low acidity by appropriate dosage of SO_2 in one or another of its various forms. The anaerobic organisms with which this section is concerned develop best at high temperatures, temperatures at which the fermenting power of the true wine yeasts begins to wane. They are most at home in a low acid medium; and they are controlled by SO_2. Some of them, given the chance, will make the wine bitter, others will make it oily and ropy, others (the mannitic ferments) give it a sickish sweet-bitter taste, the notorious taste that in California is called "mousiness," which makes the wine absolutely undrinkable, and which was the bane of the California wine-makers in the years immediately following repeal: it is a menace in all hot wine countries. Another malady, called *tourne*, is as bad. Wines infected with this disease have a thoroughly disagreeable aroma and flavor, somewhat recalling acetic fermentation, but if possible more disagreeable, and they frequently show mousiness as well. Along with these disagreeable symptoms the wine also turns gassy.

Once any one of these bacterial diseases has gained the upper hand, nothing can be done about it. The wine should be dumped. They are rarely troublesome in Eastern wines.

Casse. This difficulty is caused by the oxydases present in dead-ripe grapes, and in grapes that have been touched by rot or the other mildew diseases. The oxydases are responsible for the familiar darkening of fruits, say of apples or peaches, when they are cut, and of fruit juices. This they do as catalysts, by causing the oxidation of certain substances in the fresh must or wine. The characteristic darkening is accompanied by a persistent haze and an oxidized flavor. Some wines are more subject to casse than others. Again, the proper treatment is preventive: the exclusion of air, and the judicious use of sulphur dioxide, with its power to counteract oxidative reactions. The way to test a young wine's tendency to casse is to draw off a small quantity in a glass and leave it in the open for twenty-four hours. If it darkens or shows haze, casse is a thing to watch out for. But if the subsequent handling of the wine is correct,[2] the casse will never have an opportunity to develop.

Metal Pickup. Now for the illnesses of a chemical rather than a biological origin.

The difficulties caused by metal contamination—what is called *metal pickup* by wine-makers—are, ironically, a direct result of labor-saving improvements in wine-making technique. So long as wine-making equipment was crude and simple, the symptoms now associated with metal pickup were rarely encountered. There is none when grapes are crushed by human feet or wooden rollers, handled in wooden tubs and buckets, pressed in wooden presses, stored in wooden casks, and bottled direct from the cask through wooden spigots. Metal pickup, as one might suspect, is a consequence of the use of metal—metal crushers, presses, pipelines, spigots, and bungs and manholes—metal liquid-handling machinery of all sorts. Metal pickup causes more trouble in modern wine-making than any other forms of accident or disease.

We must remember that must and wine are acid solutions. Acid combines with metals—with some metals more than others—to form certain metallic compounds, or salts. These salts, which are not normally present in wine, have a tendency to act up in ways that adversely affect the quality of wine, even though they may be present in very small concentrations.[3] Specifically, they give rise, under various circumstances, to a persistent cloudiness in the wine

---

[2] That is, if the wine is always lightly sulphured when racked, and containers are kept full.

[3] As little as five parts per million of iron or .3 to .5 p.p.m. of copper may give trouble.

which ruins its attractive appearance and imparts to it a certain bitterness. Furthermore, the appearance of this persistent cloudiness is unpredictable, and most frequently and inconveniently takes place after the wine is bottled.

The two most troublesome metals, so far as the development of such cloudiness is concerned, are iron and copper. The acids of wine react eagerly with iron. For that reason, must and wine should not be allowed to come in contact with it. They react somewhat less readily with copper. Iron and copper should therefore, if used, be coated with an acid-resistant material—vitreous enamel, one of the many plastic coatings available, or a plating of one of the metals that do not react readily with wine, such as tin, chromium, or silver. Or metal parts should be made entirely of a metal not susceptible to corrosion by wine, such as silver, certain aluminum alloys, and certain stainless-steel alloys. The wine industry in general is moving toward the use of stainless steel.

In small-scale wine-making, metal pickup rarely presents a problem, because small-scale wine-making, so far as equipment is concerned, is always relatively primitive. If the small crusher or press does happen to have certain metal parts that come in contact with the must or wine, it is an easy matter to coat them. Or the contact is so brief that no trouble follows. Aside from these, the only source of metal contamination in small-scale wine-making is by accident— dropping into a barrel a piece of iron wire such as is used to suspend burning sulphur pastilles, using a galvanized bucket, and so on.

What is to be done if the wine-maker has reason to suspect that his wine has picked up some metal? If iron is the offender, there is a relatively easy means of forestalling difficulty. This is based on the fact that the iron salts of certain organic acids are more soluble than others, and especially the salts of citric acids. Thus, if a suspicion arises that iron has been picked up, the thing to do is to add a dose of pure citric acid at the rate of 30 grams per hectoliter [4] shortly before bottling. The effect of the citric acid is to make sure that the iron present in the wine will not precipitate in the form of a cloud.

The case of copper is more difficult. In fact there exists only one method, which is to remove the offending copper by one of several highly technical processes, which consist essentially in the precipitation of the copper. This is no field for amateurs.

Mysterious Tastes. Finally, carelessness in wine-making occasionally leads to the development of uncharacteristic odors and flavors in wine—moldy tastes, the taste of wood or cork, or even an odor of kerosene or fuel oil. Most of these tastes arrive through negligence—the use of improperly prepared cooperage, of unclean equipment, of excessively moldy fruit, and so forth, or by the exposure of wine to strong odors such as that of gasoline. If wine is spoiled in any of these ways, the wine-maker has only his own carelessness to blame. He has failed to observe the cardinal rule of cleanliness.

FALSE WINES

Piquette. No matter how thoroughly it is pressed, red-wine pomace still contains appreciable quantities of coloring mat-

[4] About 1 ounce per 20 gallons.

ter, alcohol, acid, and still-unfermented sugar. From time immemorial it has been the custom in wine-making countries to extract these desirable constituents by adding a quantity of water to the red pomace after it has been pressed, stirring water and pomace together, allowing it to stand for a few days, and pressing it again. The liquid thus obtained is of course extremely low in alcohol content (three or four per cent at most), but tart and fresh. It clears rapidly and is consumed during the months immediately following the vintage. A taste for *piquette* must be acquired. It is drunk in large quantities by farm laborers in many parts of the Old World, as it has been from the time of the Romans.

Sugar Wines. Sugar wine is a sort of sophisticated *piquette*, which also makes use of the pomace but produces a beverage more closely approaching real wine than *piquette* does. The pomace, after being pressed, is thrown back into the fermenting-vat and broken up. A sugar solution equal in quantity to the amount of wine that has been pressed off is then added to the pomace. The sugar content of this solution should be about 20 Balling,[5] or approximately the sugar content of the "normal" must. A small dose of tartaric acid (6 gm. per gallon, dissolved in a bit of warm water) is then added to keep the concoction from being too insipid. The pomace is of course full of active yeast, and when the sugar solution is added, this yeast immediately undertakes, once again, its function of helping sugar become alcohol. Within a few hours a new violent fermentation is under

[5] 1.7 pounds per gallon dissolved in ordinary tap water if the quality of the water is good, otherwise in distilled water.

way, and the new sugar wine is treated from then on ex- actly as real wine is treated.

If these directions are followed, the resulting beverage will help the amateur who is short of grapes to eke out his supply of wine with a tolerable substitute. But it should be kept separate. The sugar wine is of course much lighter in color and in body than real wine. Its manufacture by bonded wineries is strictly illegal.

CHAPTER XIII

Sparkling Wine

Many people use the terms *sparkling wine* and *champagne* interchangeably. Some do it in ignorance, others know better. Champagne is a sparkling wine, but not every sparkling wine is champagne. Let us agree that true champagne is wine made from Pinot Noir and Pinot Blanc grapes grown within the French viticultural district of Champagne and rendered sparkling by fermentation in bottle. Other sparkling wines fail to qualify as champagne by reason of the grapes from which they were made, the region where they were made, or the method of manufacture.

1. *Méthode Champenoise.* These are wines made according to the traditional champagne process, but made elsewhere and usually of other grapes. Many are famous in their own right, such as sparkling Saumur, sparkling Vouvray, the Italian Asti Spumante, certain sparkling Moselles and Rhine wines, sparkling Burgundy, and the best so-called American champagnes.[1]

2. *Bulk Fermented Wines.* These wines derive their sparkle, as does champagne, as a result of fermentation. The

[1] Under U.S. law, any bottle-fermented sparkling wine is entitled to call itself "champagne." This is a sore point in Franco-American diplomacy.

difference is that these wines, which in France are said to be fermented *en cuve close,* are fermented in large pressure tanks and not in individual bottles, after which they are bottled under pressure and dressed up to look as much like champagne as possible. The process is rational, and it eliminates much hand work, and the best of these wines may be superior to second-quality true champagne.

3. *Carbonated Wines.* These are still wines that have been carbonated much as pop is carbonated. The process is cheap and rapid. If the base wine is good, such wine can be very agreeable. In the United States carbonated wine must be so identified on the bottle.

The *méthode champenoise* calls for more work than does the making of still wines, and for certain special equipment. Before attempting it, one should be familiar with the making of still wines. Nevertheless, the elements of the process are simple, and the necessary manipulations call for no dexterity that cannot be quickly acquired. Nor does the method require to be undertaken on large quantities of wine. Five gallons of good still wine will yield 25 bottles of sparkling. As a Christmas present a bottle of well-made sparkling wine is at least as acceptable as a handkerchief.

The rudiments of the method may be described quite briefly. A white wine is fermented out absolutely dry as though to make still wine, after the fashion described in Chapter IX. The wine is racked from its gross lees at the end of November or in December. It is then stored in a cool place, in order to hasten clearing. During the succeeding two or three months it is given several other careful rackings. At the end of February or in March, or even April, a measured quantity of sugar is dissolved in this wine; and the wine is then bottled, corked, and tied or wired. With the coming of warm weather a new fermentation begins, and the dose of sugar is converted into alcohol and carbon dioxide. But the gas, instead of being allowed to escape, is held in by the cork. A sediment is inevitably produced during this bottle fermentation. As the wine clears, this sediment gradually gathers along the side of the bottle on which it is lying. With the return of cold weather in the following winter the bottles are inverted, and by a series of manipulations the sediment is caused to settle on the inside end of the cork. When this has been done, the bottle is carefully disgorged in such fashion that all sediment is blown out along with the cork, but without blowing out the wine. A dose of liqueur composed of sugar dissolved in wine or wine and brandy is then added to the bottle, and it is re-corked, rewired, and binned to await the will of the drinker.

So much for the synopsis. Now for the details, and if at first glance these seem somewhat too plentiful, let it be borne in mind that they are placed here not to add complexity to the synopsis, but to clarify it. The synopsis really covers the whole ground. In general the descriptions will follow the practice of the domestic wine-makers and small proprietors of the Champagne district itself, with, for the sake of variety, an occasional reference to the practices of the great Champagne houses.

2: THE WINE

Wines to be rendered sparkling must be absolutely sound. It is unwise to use a wine about which there is the slightest doubt, because the bitterness of disappointment increases in accordance with the amount of work expended. Nor will every sound white wine necessarily make a good sparkling wine: it should conform to certain general specifications:

1. The wine should be light in body, with an alcoholic content between 10 and 11 per cent. A wine of less than 10 per cent does not readily absorb the carbon dioxide produced during subsequent bottle fermentation. A wine of more than 11 per cent may not re-ferment satisfactorily.

2. The wine should have an acidity of about .8 per cent to assure a sound refermentation and to give vivacity to the finished sparkling wine.

3. The wine should contain tannin, partly to assure a good clarification before refermentation and partly to ensure against cloudiness after refermentation. Thus wine that is to be rendered sparkling should receive a dose of 5 to 6 gm. per hectoliter [2] of tannic acid at the time of its original fermentation.

4. The wine should be thoroughly clarified and stabilized, which is to say that the malo-lactic fermentation has run its course, tartrates have been eliminated by a good midwinter chilling, and the wine has been fined to assure brilliance.

3: THE BOTTLE FERMENTATION

In short, we begin with a relatively finished wine—clear, sound, clean to the nose, and fresh to the palate. And the time to begin is the spring after fermentation. The French

[2] One hectoliter equals 26.42 gallons.

have a term, *tirage*, which stands for the bottle fermentation and the sequence of operations leading up to it. This sequence consists in blending the wines,[3] testing the *cuvée*, preparing the *liqueur de tirage* or sugar dose, preparing the yeast starter, adding the liqueur and the yeast to the *cuvée*, placing in bottles, corking, wiring, and cellar treatment.

Blending. In the Champagne district it is the blending of base wine from different parts of the district that accounts for the difference between one famous brand and another. The American amateur has no set standards to go by, at least in the beginning. He can forget about blending. Later he may wish to experiment; and if so, there is one French practice that he may find useful. This is the practice of blending his base wine with not more than one fourth of an older wine—what the French call *vin de réserve*. This helps to achieve uniform characteristics from year to year, improves the bouquet, helps the wine to retain its sparkle, and generally assists in rounding off the rough edges.

Testing the Cuvée. The wine, whether blended or not, must be dosed with a quantity of sugar sufficient to make the *mousse*, or sparkle, before it is placed in bottles. The dosage of sugar depends partly on the composition of the wine and partly on the strength of *mousse*, or amount of bubble, that the wine-maker wants to impart. This is the time, then, for an analysis of the wine. The usual tests at this time are for *alcoholic content, total acidity*, and *sugar content*.

The tests should confirm (a) that alcoholic content is between 10 and 11 per cent by volume, (b) that the total acidity is between 7.5 and 9 gm. per liter as tartaric, and

[3] A blend of wines to be rendered sparkling is called a *cuvée*.

(c) that the wine has no residue of fermentable sugar. The tests for alcoholic content and total acidity are made as described on pp. 156 and 127. The chemical test for residual sugar is altogether too complicated for the amateur. He relies on the taste test: if the wine is perceptibly sweet, he does not use it for sparkling wine. In the Champagne district a wine containing residual sugar of more than 4 gm. per liter (.4 per cent) is never used.

It is of course desirable to make sure that there is adequate tannin in the wine. But this test, too, is complicated. The amateur can play safe, in skipping this test, by adding a very small dose of tannin at this point (.5 gm. per hectoliter).

Preparing the Liqueur de Tirage. The sugar that causes the fermentation, and hence the bubbles, is added as a liqueur, or syrup. If insufficient sugar is added, not much fermentation can take place in bottle; hence there won't be much sparkle. If too much sugar is added, the fermentation is too strong and the bottles blow up. The character of the resulting sparkling wine depends largely on the accuracy with which this dose is measured.

The average champagne, with a *mousse*, or sparkle, that is vigorous, plentiful, and long-lasting once the bottle is opened, is fermented to a pressure of between 4 and 5 atmospheres.[4] Occasionally a champagne may be fermented to a pressure of 6 atmospheres; but in such cases the *mousse* is altogether too lively for the pleasure and comfort of most consumers. The champagnes called *crémant* (creamy) are

[4] The unit of measurement of the pressure of gases is the *atmosphere,* which is the equivalent of the weight of a mercury column 1 centimeter in diameter and 30 inches high, at the sea level at London, at a temperature of 0° C. Also, a pressure of 1.033 kg. per cm².

somewhat less bumptious; their pressure is usually between 2 and 3 atmospheres. Prudent amateurs content themselves with a sparkling wine that is *crémant*.

The computations by which the wineries arrive at the exact dosage of sugar which they propose to give their wines are complicated in the extreme and take into account every conceivable factor. Luckily there is a simple rule that is sufficiently accurate for the amateur: *four grams of sugar per liter of wine yield one atmosphere of pressure by fermentation in the bottle.* The application is simple. Assume that the amount of wine to be rendered sparkling is 20 gallons (or 75.7 liters [5]), and that a sparkling wine with a pressure of 4 atmospheres is sought. The necessary amount of sugar is 75.7 (liters) × 4 (grams of sugar to yield 1 atmosphere) × 4 (atmospheres) equals 1211.2 grams of sugar, or 43.7 ounces. [6]

The liqueur, or syrup, is prepared by dissolving cane sugar in a suitable quantity of wine. If the liqueur is prepared more than a day in advance of its use, old wine should be used; new wine usually contains yeast cells, which promptly attack the sugar. Let us assume, however, that the wine-maker has no old wine for this purpose. If 20 gallons are to be bottled, about 3 gallons are drawn off the day before bottling, into a clean five-gallon bottle. The measured quantity of sugar (43.7 oz. in this case) is added to this wine and shaken thoroughly. The bottle is shaken sev-

[5] One gallon equals 3.785 liters. One gram equals .0353 ounces.
[6] Some domestic wine-makers use even more of a rule of thumb than this; year in and year out, they add 2½ ounces of sugar for every gallon of wine to be rendered sparkling. This yields a *mousse* of about 5 atmospheres of pressure, which is about all that a second-hand champagne bottle ought to be made to stand.

Nine-hundred-gallon oak ovals. Note door for entering for cleaning. Old hand press in foreground. (Courtesy Charles Krug Winery)

Attaching hose for racking new wine from storage cask. (Courtesy Taylor Wine Company)

Red wine fermenting room showing sequence of vintage operations. Counter clockwise (1) Fermenter being filled with crushed and ... from ... (2) worker ... for ... in active fermentation; (4) worker punching down the cap of a red wine fermenter; (5) worker holding hose in process of recirculating fermenting must through a cooling unit. (Courtesy Inglenook Vine...

Hydraulic wine press, 16-bushel capacity. Truck containing filled press basket is rolled over hydraulic cylinder, which raises truck against block to provide pressure. Home-made adaptation of conventional French pattern. Note GI gasoline tank use as hydraulic fluid reservoir. (Boordy Vineyard)

BELOW: Stacking newly bottled champagne prior to secondary fermentation. (Courtesy Urbana Wine Company)

This unusual photograph was taken by Muybridge, of San Francisco, a contemporary of Brady, the great Civil War photographer, in the early 1870's. The scene was the Buena Vista (originally Haraszthy) Vineyard, and it shows the principal operations in finishing "brut" champagne. Essentially the operations are no different today. (L to R) The men are (1) disgorging; (2) removing a stubborn cork; (3) adding the dosage; (4) inserting the finish cork; (5) admiring the finished product; (6) wiring the cork; (7) putting foil cap in place. (Courtesy Buena Vista Vineyard)

Small portable crusher-stemmer of European type. Designed for hand operation but fitted with gear reduction motor. (Boordy Vineyard)

eral times, to make sure that the sugar dissolves completely. The wine should under no circumstances be heated. When the sugar is thoroughly dissolved, this liqueur is put away in a cool place until the time for mixing it into the bulk of the wine.

If the amateur uses old wine for making his liqueur, he must make sure that it is sound and of good quality, and he must take account of the amount to be so used when he makes his sugar calculations. If, for instance, he is planning to bottle 20 gallons and to use 2 gallons of old wine for his liqueur, he must calculate the quantity of sugar on the basis of 22 gallons.

Preparing the Yeast Starter. Wine cannot be rendered sparkling in bottles, of course, unless some cells of yeast are present to attack the added sugar. Such yeast is almost invariably present in the new wine, even though it has been racked two or three times and fined once and seems quite clear. Until Pasteur had demonstrated the role of yeasts in fermentation, the yeast cells naturally present in the wines were relied upon entirely. But every now and then a batch of wine "stuck"—that is, refused to ferment in bottles. The old champagne-makers had no rational explanation for this. The modern champagne-makers know that a "stuck" batch is evidence of work too well done. The wine has fermented so completely and has been cleared so perfectly that no yeast cells remain to carry on the work in bottle. They circumvent the danger of this by adding to the wine, shortly before it is placed in bottles, an actively fermenting starter of yeast.

The preparation of yeast starters during the vintage season is relatively easy because of the accessibility of plenty of fresh must in which to develop the yeast culture. But in late winter no fresh must is available. A yeast starter for bottle fermentation is therefore prepared in a special way. The simplest way to illustrate the technique of preparing it is to consider a specific example. Assume, again, that 20 gallons of wine are to be bottled. Put 1½ gallons of the wine into a two-gallon or three-gallon bottle. To this add a pure culture of wine yeast and mix thoroughly. Then add 2 ounces of cane sugar dissolved in a small quantity of water. It also helps to add to this a few grams of phosphate yeast food, though this is not necessary. The bottle should then be shaken thoroughly again, lightly stoppered with absorbent cotton, and put in a moderately warm place. It should be shaken twice a day, in order to provide the yeast with plenty of air. Signs of yeast growth and fermentation should appear shortly, and in two or three days the starter will be in full fermentation and ready to use. If for some reason the bottling is delayed, another 2 ounces of sugar must be added at the end of three or four days to keep the yeasts at work.

If all this seems pretty complicated, some comfort is to be had from the fact that for several centuries champagne-makers got along quite well without yeast starters. Only rarely does the bottled wine fail to contain sufficient yeast to start the bottle fermentation.

Bottles. Champagne bottles are specially made to withstand high pressures; a first-quality new champagne bottle can easily withstand a pressure of 8 atmospheres, though in practice it is never called on to do so. But bottles subjected to a strain, especially a fluctuating strain (and of course the pressure in a bottle of champagne varies every time the barometer or the thermometer moves up or down), become fatigued, just as steel that is subjected to strain becomes fatigued. A second-hand champagne bottle cannot stand a pressure so great as a new one. In France many manufacturers of the cheaper brands of sparkling wines use second-hand bottles, and they usually reduce their pressure accordingly.

Bottles that were not originally made to stand such pressure invariably prove disappointing.[7] During prohibition many amateurs in the United States used ginger-ale and pop bottles, with only moderate success.

Bottles in which wine is to be fermented are always examined one by one, by being held up to a good light. All bottles showing bubbles in the glass or other irregularities are rejected. It is simply silly to use them, unless one enjoys the sound of exploding glassware. After being thus examined, they are always, in the Champagne district, given another test. The tester takes a bottle in each hand, by the neck, and knocks the two smartly together. If they don't break, they are good bottles; if they do, why, it is better to have them break empty than full.

The bottles are then washed and rinsed thoroughly. They should not be washed until shortly before they are to be filled.

Corks and Caps. There are many grades and qualities of cork. Second-quality cork will not do for sparkling wine because it will not hold the pressure. The standard new No. 14 champagne cork looks as though it could never be crowded into the neck of the bottle, and indeed it cannot be with the corking devices at the disposal of the amateur.

[7] Remember, too, that an exploding bottle is a very dangerous thing.

Ordinary hand corking machines of the kind that clamp or screw onto a table cannot handle them. These will, however, handle corks of the size known in the trade as No. 9 1¾ inch; and such corks will do for wines with a pressure of not more than 2 atmospheres.

In recent years a new kind of champagne bottle has been developed and is now being used by most American and some European sparkling-wine producers. It has a lip resembling that of a pop or beer bottle, and takes crown caps. Caps are used for the *tirage;* and at the time of disgorging, the cap is abandoned and a conventional champagne cork, or preformed plastic cork or another crown cap, is used for the final closure. The solution for the amateur is to scout around for some second-hand bottles of this type, and a supply of crown corks, and one of those hand beer-bottle cappers that were so popular during prohibition.

Bottling. The actual bottling may be done any time after the wine is clear, usually in early spring. The necessary dose of sugar is calculated and the *tirage* liqueur prepared one day in advance. Bottles are examined and washed and corks prepared on the day of bottling. On that day give the wine a final racking into a clean container. This moderate aeration allows the wine to absorb the oxygen necessary for the multiplication of the yeast in the wine. This is the wine's last chance to get oxygen.

As soon as the wine has been racked, add the measured dose of *tirage* liqueur (sugar syrup) and mix thoroughly.[8] Then add the yeast starter, if one is to be used, and stir it in. Wine, liqueur, and starter should be stirred at intervals for an hour or so before the actual bottling is begun. Some

[8] For the space, says one ancient authority, of a *Miserere.*

wine-makers even allow twelve hours, with occasional stir-
rings, in order to give the yeast a chance to get a hold on
the wine. During the actual bottling the wine must also be
stirred at intervals in order to keep the yeast in suspension.
Fill the bottles by siphon tube to about 1 ½ inches from the
mouth.

Corking. Sterilize the corks by bringing them just to a
boil and allowing them to stand for a half-hour. Then rinse,
drain, and keep the corks wrapped in a clean towel. Drive
corks halfway—that is, so that one half the length of the
cork protrudes from the mouth of the bottle. If caps are
used, make sure that they are solidly crimped.

Wiring. Corks must be tied or wired to keep them from
blowing out when pressure develops. Before they are tied,
they should be mushroomed or partly flattened in order to
assure a tight seal. In wineries this is done by a machine that
mushrooms the cork and fits over it a stout little metal
clamp called an *agraffe.* Small French producers use instead
a special sort of plier which not only mushrooms the cork

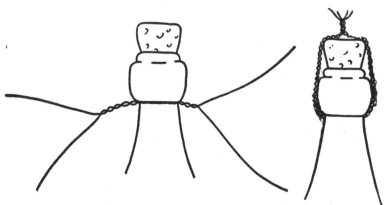

Tying champagne corks with No. 20 wire.

but keeps it that way while it is being tied. Corks may also be mushroomed pretty well with a beer capper. Use No. 20 galvanized wire for tying. The method of tying is shown in the accompanying illustration. First secure the wire around the neck of the bottle, the two open ends being twisted to form a single strand: thus in effect a stout twisted wire of two strands extends from each side of the bottle-neck. These are brought up over the cork and in turn twisted together, the final twist being embedded in the end of the cork by a whack of the pliers.

Bottle Fermentation. Stack the bottles on their sides as soon as they have been corked and wired. If left standing upright, the corks will dry out and the pressure be lost. In the Champagne district the bottles are ordinarily stacked twenty tiers high, the first tier being placed on a firm base-board in which notches to receive the necks and bases of the bottles have been cut. The next tier is stacked with the necks on the bottles pointing in the opposite direction, with a lath placed along the base of the bottom tier of bottles to support them.[9] In this way each tier is made as solid as the bottom one. As each bottle is stacked, a mark is made on it with a damp chalk or thick whitewash directly over the bubble. Thus, when the bottles are restacked later, they are always replaced with the mark up. If this is not done, the sediment that is shaken up in the course of moving the bottles settles on a different part of the interior of the bot-tle. Experience is that this causes difficulty when the time for disgorging arrives. The sediment should always be al-

[9] In champagne cellars the end bottles are held in place, making vertical-side piles feasible, by a neat arrangement of wedges, made of old corks and laths. But the arrangement defies description.

lowed to settle in the same place if the bottles are moved.

Normally the bottle fermentation begins immediately. Its speed is governed partly by the amount and vigor of the yeast in the bottle and partly by the temperature at which the bottles are kept. The higher the temperature of the cellar, the faster the fermentation; but wines that ferment rapidly in bottle at relatively high temperatures may not be quite so good as those whose fermentation has been leisurely and cool. A temperature of between 60° and 77° F. is satisfactory; it should be kept as constant as possible. At 77° F. the bottle fermentation is usually completed in about three weeks; at 60° F. it may poke along for many months.

Ripening. When the bottle fermentation has been concluded, the wine is not yet ready for disgorging. The wine must first become clear, and the sediment must be given an opportunity to ripen—that is, to settle in a mass as compact and granular as possible. A loose, soft, amorphous mass of sediment is always difficult to disgorge satisfactorily. So when the fermentation is finished, the bottles are thoroughly shaken one by one, in order to stir the yeast cells to attack the last remaining particles of sugar, and then restacked for clearing (with the white mark uppermost).

The length of the ripening-period depends on several factors. French houses that specialize in superior champagnes leave their bottles in the cellar for several years, allowing the wines to mature and the sediment to ripen very gradually. If that is done, the bottles are shaken and restacked several times a year. Those who make the cheaper champagnes have ways of speeding the process tremendously. Thus, by subjecting the bottles to a rapid fermentation, then following this with a period of prolonged chilling, they are able to produce finished champagne in a period of only two months from the time of bottling to the final labeling. Wine made in November may be all tricked out and ready to drink by the time it is six months old.

Amateurs usually strike a mean. After the shaking and restacking, which usually takes place toward the end of summer, say in August, they give the wine no attention until the coming of cold weather. Then, usually fairly early in November if there is a prospect of several crisp days, the bottles are chilled by being stacked under cover outdoors or in an unheated shed or garage. Below-freezing temperatures will do no harm to the wine, since the freezing-point of wine is considerably lower than that of water. This chilling further ripens the sediment and rids the wine of cream of tartar, which might otherwise precipitate after the wine had been entirely finished. The chilling may be omitted, however.

Remuage. When cool weather has arrived for good, the wine has cleared perfectly, and the sediment has settled in a compact streak along the under side of the bottle. It is time to begin the operation that the French call *remuage* (literally, stirring or twirling), for which the English "riddling" is a poor equivalent. This consists in placing the bottles, at an angle, neck down, in a special frame or rack and by a series of gentle jogs or shakings causing the sediment gradually to slip down until it has settled on the inner end of the cork.

The racks used for this purpose in the Champagne district are very solidly built, and the holes in which the necks of the bottles are held are accurately drilled. Notice especially the horizontal strip of wood which is fastened behind, and just above, each row of holes. This is important, be-cause it allows the manipulator of the bottles to adjust the bottle angle. If the neck of the bottle is barely thrust into

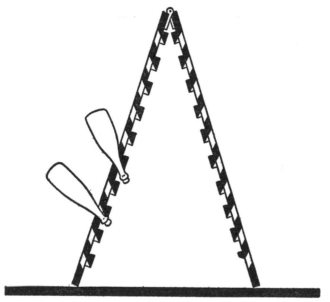

Pupitre, or clearing rack, for Champagne, showing how bottles are gradually brought to their point.

the hole, the bottle is held at an angle just above the hori-zontal. If the neck of the bottle is thrust in as far as it can go, the bottle is held firmly in a position nearly vertical.

Such racks are expensive. A fairly satisfactory substitute is a simple latticework forming diamond-shaped holes. The lattice must be very rigid and should have the wooden crosspieces behind each row of holes.

To begin the *remuage*, the bottles are placed in the rack at an angle barely above the horizontal. Each bottle, before being put in its hole, is very thoroughly shaken until no sediment whatever clings to the bottle's side. If some of the sediment persists in adhering—forms a "mask," as the champagne-makers say—it is useless to put that bottle in the rack. It must be set aside and given special treatment to loosen the mask.

These adherent masks are caused by the development of sticky or gummy, rather than granular, sediment. It is to prevent these that such pains were taken to clear the wine before bottling it. A wine that has received its sufficient dose of tannin and has been cleared of its albuminous matter by fining is not likely to develop this difficulty.[1] The traditional, and for the amateur the only available, method of dislodging the mask is to shake the bottle very violently, then to hold it in the lap and tap the bottle repeatedly with a light metal rod, then to shake it again, and then to tap some more, and so on until the mask gives up in sheer disgust and lets go. It is the part of caution to wear goggles and gloves for this little task. The wineries have special machines for dislodging the mask. A bottle is strapped into place and by means of a series of eccentrics is given a violent and prolonged rocking and shaking of several hundred jolts a minute. Rare and tenacious is the mask that can withstand this kind of treatment. When the mask is finally loosened, the bottle may be placed with the others in the rack.

The bottles are allowed to rest in the racks until the sediment has settled once more and the wine is perfectly clear. Then the actual *remuage* begins. The protruding base of the bottle is marked with damp chalk at the point which

---

[1] In France, special *"colles,"* or fining materials, have been developed for introducing into the wine at the time of the *tirage*.

would be twelve o'clock if the base were a clock. Then the first bottle is grasped by the base, pulled out of its hole a trifle, rocked gently, turned clockwise one eighth of a turn, and dropped back into the hole with a gentle jar. The white mark enables the operator to give all bottles the same degree of turn.

In two or three days the process is repeated, each bottle being given another one-eighth turn. That brings the mark on each bottle to the three-o'clock position. The bottles are jogged a third time in a few more days, and so on. And with each jog the bottle is brought into a position a little more nearly vertical. This lifting of the bottle toward the vertical position must be done gradually; otherwise the sediment is apt to float off into the wine and cloud it.

The result of this combination of jogging the bottle, turning it slightly, and inclining it a little more steeply is that the sediment each time slips down a little toward the cork. The *remueur* in the great champagne cellars attains an astounding proficiency, giving as many as twenty-five thousand bottles their fractional turn each day. The succession of little clicks as the bottles drop back into their holes is as steady in a champagne cellar as the ticking of a clock. Ordinarily in these cellars the *remueurs* grasp a bottle in each hand—the first and the fourth in a row—thus doing two bottles simultaneously. Then they do the second and fifth, the third and sixth, and so on.[2]

The chief precaution to observe is not to allow the sediment in the bottle to creep too far up the side. That is, when the bottle is given its turn, the sediment should slip

[2] The *pupitre*, or rack, normally holds sixty bottles on each side—in ten rows of six bottles each.

not only toward the cork, but back to the six-o'clock position. Under no circumstances should the sediment be allowed to creep, with successive turnings, above the nine-o'clock mark; for then, with the next turning, it will float free of the side of the bottle, cloud the wine, and force the *remueur* to begin all over again. If the sediment shows a disposition to creep up the side of the bottle, the bottle should be given the jog without the turn. If the sediment were perfectly homogeneous and of the same specific gravity, the job would be simple; the trouble is that many different substances go to make up the sediment of wine. Some of these, such as the crystals of cream of tartar, are heavy and sink quickly; others have almost the same specific gravity as the wine and sink with difficulty. The likelihood of having to deal with these light cloudy sediments is minimized if the wine is properly prepared before bottling.

By the time each bottle has been given eight jogs and turns, the white mark will have traveled all the way around to its original twelve-o'clock position; barring accidents, the sediment will have slipped well down toward the cork. It is then possible to increase each turn to one sixth—that is, from twelve o'clock to two o'clock, from two o'clock to four o'clock and so on. If the sediment is unusually well-behaved, the bottles may even be given a full quarter turn each time.

At last, in a period varying from twenty days to several months, according to the skill of the operator and the amenability of the sediment, all of the sediment will have been brought down to the inner end of the cork. It should then remain in the racks without further treatment until the time for disgorging and the final preparation of the wine for use. In commercial establishments the wines may be left thus for many years,[3] for the bottles are not ordinarily disgorged until just before shipment. The longer the bottles are thus left on their points, the more compact the sediment becomes and the more successful the operation of disgorging.

4: FINAL TREATMENT

The term *brut* is loosely used on the labels of champagnes and other sparkling wines. Ordinarily it is taken to mean unsweet, or a few shades drier than "dry," "*sec*," or "extra dry." Actually, the word means rough, raw, unfinished; and in wine-making it is used technically to mean sparkling wine that has undergone bottle fermentation and has been cleared of its sediment, but has had no doctoring.

The taste for a really *brut* sparkling wine must be acquired. With some allowance for exaggeration, the celebrated remark of the Danish Prince Aage, who complained that an evening of champagne-drinking was like an evening spent rushing from house to house licking dusty windowpanes, applies to *brut* wines. For that reason sparkling wines are customarily dosed in the finishing process with a liqueur composed of cane sugar and wine (and sometimes brandy). The amount of such *dosage* is fixed by popular demand and regional preferences.[4] "Extra dry" means a sugar content of between one and two per cent.

[3] Or removed from the racks, to make way for a new lot, and stacked *en masse* in bins, cork down, several bottles high.

[4] In spite of Prince Aage, there appears to be a growing taste in our country for *brut* champagnes containing about .5 per cent sugar.

This sweetening liqueur does not give rise to another bottle fermentation because, if the disgorging is carried out successfully, no yeast cells will remain in the bottle, and because any remaining yeasts are enfeebled by lack of oxygen and a shortage of the necessary phosphates, and also because the fermentation in bottle will have raised the alcoholic content high enough to discourage any further fermentation.

Preparing the Dosage. Commercial establishments ordinarily use a quantity of brandy in their liqueur because the vicissitudes of a bottle of champagne are unpredictable; the additional alcohol helps to strengthen its constitution. Also, some markets demand a champagne of high alcoholic content. The amateur practically never uses brandy in preparing his liqueur. He uses only old wine and cane sugar. A wine of two years is satisfactory; a wine three or four years old is better.

The *dosage* liqueur should be as concentrated as possible; the more concentrated it is, the less one needs to add. One may dissolve twenty-four ounces of sugar in a quart of wine at room temperature without difficulty. It should be dissolved not by heating, but by repeatedly shaking the bottle. The bottle should be kept well corked in order to keep out yeast cells or other contamination.

Disgorging. Disgorging is the most ticklish of all the operations involved in making sparkling wines, and the amateur ordinarily loses a few bottles at his first try. Industrially, the job is subdivided; that is, one man actually blows the cork and sediment, another adds the dose of liqueur, a third corks, a fourth ties or wires, and a fifth inspects. But the amateur is likely to have to carry through the whole sequence of operations on one bottle at a time; he cannot disgorge a group of bottles, then dose them, then cork them, for they will lose their pressure unless they are handled rapidly.

The problem of disgorging is to remove the cork, and with it every bit of sediment, and in the process to lose a minimum of wine and gas. Amateurs usually choose for this operation a cold day or evening several weeks after the conclusion of the *remuage*. During the intervening period the bottles have been standing in the rack neck down, with all of the sediment accumulated on the inner end of the cork.

Several hours before the beginning of the disgorging the bottles are placed outdoors or else in a freezer. The colder the wine, the more carbon dioxide will be held in solution and the less pressure will be lost during the disgorging. While being chilled, the bottles should of course stay neck down in ginger-ale or beer cases or in baskets.

When the bottles are as cold as they are going to become, a brine should be prepared of chipped ice or snow and coarse salt. An ordinary washtub will do for the brine, or the stationary tubs in a laundry. The chilled bottles are inserted in this brine, neck down, to a depth of around 2 ½ inches. In this, the wine next to the inner end of the cork, including the sediment deposited there, freezes into a solid plug of ice. This freezing requires from half an hour to an hour, according to the strength of the brine and the degree of the preliminary chilling.

Before beginning the work of disgorging, the equipment should all be made ready. The following items should be assembled: wire-cutting pincers; a box or small keg into which closure and ice plug may be blown; dosing liqueur, well chilled; a small ladle with good pouring lip for dosing; corks,[5] wrapped in damp cloth and ready to use; corking-machine; mushrooming device (beer-bottle capper); wires or prepared wire caps. The proper costume for the evening consists of an apron, and a glove for the left hand.

Take one of the bottles from the brine and dip the neck in a pan of warm water. This will rinse all brine from around the neck and will loosen the ice plug a little. Hold the bottle by the neck with the left hand, couching it in the crook of the left arm. The bottle should be held slanting upward and outward. It should be aimed into the keg or box, which has to be placed fairly high for the purpose.

With a pair of pincers held in the right hand, cut the wire, in the meantime keeping the index finger of your left hand securely over the end of the cork. When the wire is released, remove your finger, and the cork will blow out, carrying the ice plug and a little of the wine with it. If the bottle is held properly and the wine has been thoroughly chilled, very little wine will escape. If the cork does not blow out instantly, it should be loosened gently with the right hand or with a pair of pliers held in the right hand. Then it will blow. *The bottle should be held constantly at an angle of forty-five degrees, never vertical.*

As soon as the cork and ice plug have been blown, the wine should be dosed with the liqueur. It is best to have a small ladle which holds just the determined quantity of liqueur, so that no time is lost in measuring. A dose of half an ounce is ample for the average taste, and many use less. The wine will have a tendency to foam out of the bottle

[5] Or crown caps, if corks aren't to be used.

as the dose is poured in. This foaming is minimized if the liqueur is very cold and if the bottle is rotated very gently as it is poured in. *If the bottle is not held on a slant,* the foaming will be much more violent.

If a great deal of wine is lost in the disgorging, enough wine from an already opened bottle may be introduced to bring it to the required level. In the large wineries both the dosing and the introduction of enough plain wine to fill the bottle are done by a machine that operates automatically.

As soon as the dose has been introduced, the bottle should be corked. In order to minimize the time, it is a good idea to have a cork in the machine before beginning the disgorging of a bottle. The cork is then mushroomed and wired.

The work is done when the bottle, having been securely corked and wired, is shaken to make a thorough distribution of the liqueur. The wine ought to have a month in the cellar before it is drunk, but from then on, the only requirement is an appropriate occasion.

5: WINES MADE IN CLOSED CONTAINERS

The process just described at length is the true *méthode champenoise,* by which the superior sparkling wines are traditionally made. But there are other and simpler methods. One of these differs chiefly in the fact that the wine is made to sparkle, not in individual bottles, but in large containers—*"en cuve close."* These substantial tanks are fitted with pressure gauges, safety valves, and elaborate refrigerating equipment; so, as soon as the bottle fermentation has been concluded, the wine may be chilled almost to its freezing-point and kept at this low temperature as long as the wine-maker deems desirable. Thus the manufacturing process may be closely regulated from start to finish. The wines thus made are bottled under pressure, carbon dioxide being introduced into the tank to compensate for the wine withdrawn.[6]

This method is merely the sophisticated younger brother of a method that some of the more nimble-witted French peasants have been using for a long time. The method is simplicity itself. The only special equipment is a very strong barrel, such as a beer barrel.

After the wine is made in the fall, it is given one or two rackings—a fining, too, if the wine-maker cares to take the trouble. Then it is poured into the barrel, and a measured dose of sugar that has been dissolved in a little water or wine is poured in after it and thoroughly mixed. The barrel is then tightly bunged, the bung being further secured with a metal strap or wire. In the spring, fermentation starts up in the barrel, and the wine acquires its sparkle. The barrel gets no attention whatever until the following winter, when, just before bottling time, it is put outdoors and given a prolonged and severe chilling. Great care is taken not to disturb the sediment in the bottom of the barrel. The wine, very cold, is then siphoned direct from the barrel into bottles.

[6] But the use of carbon dioxide is forbidden in commercial wineries in this country; nitrogen or air is used instead, to the detriment of quality. It is to be hoped that the authorities will presently come to their senses on this point.

The bung should be removed carefully, for, despite the absorptive power of the cold wine, there will still be an excess of pressure in the barrel, and the bung is apt to blow out pretty violently and some of the wine foam out behind it. The wine is siphoned with a glass tube just long enough to clear the sediment in the barrel, the tube being fitted into a rubber stopper that contains a second hole to allow the entrance of air into the barrel as the wine is withdrawn. The glass tube has an L at the top, so that a rubber tube may be fitted to it.

This is a rough-and-ready method. Quite a bit of the wine's pressure is lost during the bottling. Sometimes a little sediment comes over with the wine. Sometimes strange things in the way of renewed fermentation happen after the wine has been placed in bottle. But normally the sediment behaves fairly well and the wine is satisfactorily clear. And in any case the method has the merit of simplicity. It is also amenable to variations, especially in regard to the dosing of sugar. One may avoid the addition of sugar entirely by placing the wine in its barrel before the first violent fermentation is concluded and while it still contains a considerable percentage of grape sugar. Or one may deliberately add an overdose, so that at bottling time the wine will have reached its limit of alcoholic content and still contain a roughly predetermined quantity of unfermented sugar. Or one may bottle the wine *brut* and treat one's friends to the windowpane sensation, or one may place plain granulated sugar or a dose of liqueur in each bottle before it is filled from the barrel, taking a chance that fermentation will not begin again once the corks are in.

6: SPARKLING "BURGUNDY"

As most people know, the best Burgundies are not the sparkling Burgundies.[7] There is so large a demand for the great still Burgundies of the Côte d'Or, and so small a supply, that there is little incentive to make them sparkle.

Not only that; very few sparkling Burgundies are, properly speaking, red wine at all. For reasons made sufficiently clear in the preceding chapters, red wines almost invariably throw down a considerable sediment after they are placed in bottle, no matter how long they have been stored in large containers. So, even after being disgorged, true red wines which have been made to sparkle would continue to throw down sediment. And sediment is definitely out of place in a bottle of sparkling wine. So sparkling Burgundies are usually made from a rosé wine. To provide more color, the final sweetening liqueur is made with a deeply colored red wine instead of a white. Approximately twenty grams of pure citric acid are added to every gallon of liqueur. The citric acid helps to keep the coloring matter in solution and thus prevents the formation of sediment.

7: VINS PÉTILLANTS

Many wines not properly classified as sparkling nevertheless contain small quantities of carbon dioxide in solution,

[7] There are of course both red and white sparkling Burgundies; the white resemble champagnes and are usually made by the champagne method. This brief discussion is confined to red sparkling Burgundies.

so that when they are uncorked they tend to bubble a little, very gently and prettily, in the glass. Some Vouvray is of that type. This characteristic is sought after in the Swiss white wines. Such wines are obtained by making white wine after the usual manner, but without any rackings at all, and bottling in late winter or early spring direct from the lees before the coming of warm weather. Such wine always contains a small amount of carbon dioxide in solution, enough to provide the desired scattering of bubbles when later it is served. Only wines that have fallen bright spontaneously are suitable for this purpose.

8: CARBONATED WINES

A number of artificially carbonated wines are on the American market. If the wine from which they are made is of good quality, they can be agreeable. But as the only object in making such carbonated wines is to make a cheap imitation, usually the basic wine is of inferior quality, yielding an inferior final product.

The homemade counterpart to these is sparkling wine made from a sweetened still wine, into each bottle of which has been dropped a small chunk of frozen carbon dioxide—dry ice, as it is called. This was a fairly popular trick during the latter, and more sophisticated, days of prohibition; but since most dry ice is made, not to consume, but to refrigerate, the part of caution is evidently to find out whether one's dry ice is chemically pure. I am assured that in thus charging wine the dry ice may be inserted much more conveniently if it is first placed in a gelatin capsule. But to paraphrase Mr. Pope, the proper study of a chapter on wine-making is wine, and before this one degenerates into a discourse on powders and pills, perhaps it had better be drawn to a close.

CHAPTER XIV

Sweet Wines

W e have been concerned up to this point almost entirely with dry wines, either still or sparkling. There remains the matter of sweet wines, all of which fall into one or another of two categories. There are the unfortified or natural sweet wines, which derive their alcoholic content entirely by fermentation and in which a portion of the sugar of the must remains unfermented. The alcoholic content of these wines is never more than 16 per cent, and usually falls between 12 and 14 per cent. Then there are the fortified sweet wines, which contain notable amounts of sugar and which derive their alcoholic content partly by fermentation and partly by the addition of spirit. Their precise alcoholic content is determined by the quantity of spirit poured into them, is hence controlled by the wine-maker and in practice ranges from 18 to 20 per cent.

UNFORTIFIED SWEET WINES

If a wine is fermented in the normal fashion, but the yeasts abandon their work before all of the sugar has been converted into alcohol, the result is a sweet wine. An unfortified sweet wine is produced, therefore, under one or the other of two conditions: (1) the must under fermentation contains so high a proportion of sugar that the yeasts are unable to cope with it all,[1] or (2) the yeasts are called off before they have finished their task of converting all available sugar into alcohol.

Very few grape varieties, even when fully ripened, develop so much sugar that the yeasts cannot ferment it all. Still, there are some that do—all of them vinifera varieties which are grown, or may be grown, in California. Heading the list are the various members of the tribe of Muscats, which normally in California develop a sugar content of 34 to 36 per cent and quite frequently show 38 per cent or higher. The commonest of these, in California, is the Muscat of Alexandria: others, well adapted and superior, but very little grown, are Muscat de Frontignan, Muscat Noir, and Muscat Canelli. There are a few other varieties which, if allowed to overripen, will produce truly natural sweet wines that are superior to the light sweet Muscat wines: Sauvignon Blanc, Sémillon, Grenache, Maccabeo, Malvasia, Mission.

The vinification of natural sweet wines differs very little from that of dry wines. The steps are: (1) crushing; (2) pressing; (3) addition of metabisulphite to the must; (4) addition of yeast starter; (5) control of temperature during fermentation. A cool, slow fermentation is encouraged, and when the fermentation slackens noticeably the wine is racked immediately and dosed with SO_2.[2] The sulphuring

---

[1] Remember that yeasts will not usually continue their work in a solution containing more than 14 per cent alcohol.

[2] 3 gm. per 5 gallons.

has the dual object of stopping further fermentation by the yeasts and of protecting the new sweet wine from spoilage by harmful organisms. The usual rackings follow, each racking being accompanied by a protective dose of SO_2 in the form of metabisulphite.[3] Sweet wine almost invariably requires clarification by fining, 3 gm. of gelatin and 2.5 gm. of tannin for every 5 gallons of wine.

In making sweet wine of the blue vinifera grapes such as Grenache or Mission, the must may be fermented either red-wine fashion (on the skins) or white-wine fashion. Sweet red wines from Grenache acquire the aroma known as *rancio*, which is the characteristic aroma of port wines.

The sugar content of a natural sweet wine varies, of course, in accordance with the natural sweetness of the grapes. It may be anywhere from 3 to 10 per cent. If it is less than 3 per cent, the impression is likely to be that of a wine which started out to be dry but couldn't quite make it.

The most admired of the natural sweet wines are not, as a matter of fact, such wines as have just been described, but wines made from grapes that have been allowed to grow overripe under very special conditions—from grapes which, to be blunt about it, have been allowed to rot a little. These are especially the great Sauternes of France, of which Château Yquem is the model, and the *Trockenbeeren Auslese* and *Spätlese* wines of the Rhine and Moselle valleys of Germany. What happens in the case of these wines is that in late autumn an unattractive gray mold, *Botrytis cinerea*, attacks the grapes which hang slowly ripening on the vines. This *pourriture noble*, or noble rot, feeds on the

[3] 1 gm. per 5 gallons.

moisture of the grape and thus concentrates its juice and increases its relative sugar content; it also reduces the grape's acidity and does other mysterious things to the composition of the juice. When the botrytis is well advanced, the vintage begins, the workers harvesting *only* the moldy grapes. Thus several harvestings must be made before the vintage is completed. The action of the botrytis reduces the yield tremendously and increases harvesting costs, which explains why the really superior sweet wines of Sauternes and the Rhine and Moselle are so scarce and expensive. The vinification of these wines is similar to that of the other natural sweet wines. The fermentation is usually slow, and when it is finished the new wine is protected by moderate and regular doses of SO_2. The wine is fined, of course, and kept in cask at least a year before being bottled.

This description of the "noble rot" wines is included merely for the record. In California, conditions are too dry for the development of *Botrytis cinerea*. In the East, though grapes of the standard American sorts are quite frequently attacked by botrytis in wet years, the resulting rot is far from noble. Whether any of the new French hybrids will rot in a manner that can be called noble is an open question: nobody, so far as I know, has yet tried to find out.

Sugared Wines. There remains one other important method of making "natural sweet wines," which is that of building up the sugar content of the must by adding sugar.[4] Any variety of grape may be used in this way for the production of a sweet wine. The so-called "kosher" wines, for example, have a base of Concord grape juice, which is built

[4] Or grape concentrate.

up by lavish additions of sugar (and water). Other varieties, notably the French white-wine hybrids, can be used in the same fashion to produce sweet wines of rather more delicacy. The wine-maker who is interested in sweet wines will gain his end by building up the sugar content of his must to 24° Balling (or 14° Dujardin-Salleron) according to the indications of the table on page 124, and racking and sulphuring when the fermentation begins to slacken off. His wine, when stabilized, will show around 12 per cent of alcohol by volume and 4 per cent of sugar, which is approximately the analysis of a French Graves. If he prefers still sweeter wine, he may add still more sugar the next time.

FORTIFIED SWEET WINES

The wines discussed in the paragraphs above have an alcoholic content, when finished, of 12 to 14 per cent.[5] Whatever alcohol they contain was made by the action of the yeast on the sugar in the must. The fortified wines differ from these in that a part—it may be much or little—of their alcohol was added in the form of spirits, usually cheap brandy. The two great "types" are sherry and port.

Sherry. There exist in English a dozen expert accounts of the sherry-making process and its end products. Several are referred to in the bibliography. Here it is enough to put down the rudiments only—so that the reader will have

[5] Depending on the point at which the yeasts stop working of their own accord or are stopped by the addition of SO_2.

some idea what it is he is tasting when he picks up a glass of sherry, why most California sherry differs from real sherry, and how to proceed with sherry-making experiments if he is so minded.

Sherry is the wine of Jerez de la Frontera, a Spanish town about fifty miles west of Gibraltar. It is made almost entirely of two varieties of grape, Palomino and Pedro Ximenes, both of which do well in California. It comes to the market in several grades and types, of which these are the main ones: *Fino*, palest, driest, and most delicate; *Manzanilla*, similar to Fino but not quite so fine; *Amontillado*, slightly darker in color, somewhat more alcoholic usually, less delicate, often a little sweet—in short, the golden mean calculated to offend nobody even though it does not please everybody; *Oloroso, Amoroso, Brown,* or *Cream*, dark, heavy-bodied, quite alcoholic, sweet. These types are synthetic, in the sense that they result from the careful sorting-out of separate fermentings and a subsequent blending (in which aged grape syrup [6] plays a part) according to predetermined formulas.

The initial fermentation follows crushing and pressing and takes about three weeks. But the wine is not racked immediately on its conclusion; the custom is to let it clear on its gross lees. No effort is made to keep the casks filled all the way to the bung. In January these new wines are racked, and each cask receives its initial fortification. The amount of spirit added varies according to the quality of the wine, the usual rule being to fortify the best wine least; the average fortification is about 8 liters of spirit for every

---

[6] *Arropa*, which is a sort of grape concentrate, and *dulce apagado*, which is grape juice spiked with brandy.

bota, or butt, of about 480 liters.[7] After this racking the wines get no further attention until summer, when they are racked again, receive sometimes an additional fortification, and are tentatively classified. Anyone familiar with the extraordinary care given to other young wines is apt to be dismayed by the apparently careless treatment that sherry receives during these early stages. The casks lie around everywhere, in sheds and gardens, out in walled fields with the sky for a canopy, exposed to heat of noon and chill of evening. Often the casks even lack bungs. This carelessness is only apparent: the wine-makers are encouraging the growth of *Mycoderma vini*, or *flor*, or *flowers*,[8] a mold that forms a film on the surface of exposed wine, is a nuisance in the making of most wines, and for sherry has a definite affinity. The *flor* organism is related to the vinegar ferment, *Mycoderma aceti*, but does not produce the dreaded acetic acid. It largely accounts for the peculiar flavor and bouquet we associate with sherry. At any rate, the casks are left open to encourage its growth, and grow it does, in a great thick film. The wines are usually left at the mercy of the flowers until they are about a year and a half old, and are then classified again. This classification is more or less definitive. At this point they go into the cellars to take their place in the peculiar style of blending, known as the *solera* system, which ultimately produces the recognized commercial types.

Most sherries of California resemble sherry in a loose way only, because they are not made as sherries are made. The *solera* system is not used, the wine does not undergo

---

[7] Or a bit over 2 gallons for every 132 gallons.
[8] See page 182.

the *flor* fermentation,[9] and the grapes are likely to be whatever is lying around. A superficial sherry-like aroma and flavor are imported by "baking" the wine; and the baking is accomplished either by aging the wine several months in a special hot room or by introducing heating elements into the wine. The characteristic aroma and flavor are then a result of oxidation and caramelization. California sherry is in fact closer to Marsala and Madeira, both of which are "baked" wines. An amateur may approximate the "baked" effect by storing a five-gallon bottle of fortified white wine in a hot attic or next to the furnace.

Port. True port is a sweet, fortified, usually red wine grown and made in the valley of the Douro and its tributaries in Portugal. It derives its name from the town of Oporto, which lies at the mouth of the river and which is the headquarters of all the great port-shippers. In California, Australia, South Africa, Chile, Spain, Italy, France, and indeed even in Canada there are red, sweet, fortified wines that resemble port after a fashion and are so called. The wine-makers are not fooling themselves; they know that the term is inaccurate and even in some degree deceptive. But they operate under a commercial imperative. The statement of C. J. Theron, in his admirable little handbook on wine-making for South African farmers,[1] applies to all:

> In the first place the name Port, as applied to our South African wines, is wrong. . . . It should be borne in

[9] *Flor* experiments have been under way for some time, however; adaptations of the *solera* system are now coming into use; and there is a trend toward the use of Palomino and Pedro Ximenes grapes for the better grades.

[1] *Wine Making*, by C. J. Theron (Pretoria: Government Printer; 1931).

mind that they are made under totally different conditions and must therefore differ materially from the genuine Port. In the absence of a suitable name we shall continue . . . to refer to our wines of this type as Port.

In the Port district there are at least twenty important grape varieties, of which the chief are Alvarelhao, Bastardo, Donzellinho do Castello, Touriga, Tinta Francisca, Mourisco Tinto, Tinto Çao, and Cornifesto. They play no important role in the making of California ports: there the principal port varieties are the standard red-wine varieties of the Central Valley, Zinfandel and Carignane, plus to a limited extent Mission, Grenache, and Mataro. In the East the so-called port is made largely of the Concord.

But to get back to port itself and the method of vinification: it is crushed in shallow tanks, often still by foot-power, and fermented on the skins, with constant stirring for two or three days. When sugar content has been reduced by fermentation to 8 to 10 per cent, the partially fermented must is drawn off into casks in which a predetermined quantity of brandy has already been poured. The quantity of brandy must be sufficient to inhibit further fermentation, which thereupon "skids" to a stop: a wine fortified in full fermentation when it still contains a residue of 10 per cent sugar will continue to ferment long enough to reduce the sugar content by another two per cent, or to 8 per cent. The quantity of spirits added is sufficient to raise alcoholic content to 18 to 22 per cent. The essential difference between the sherry-making process and the port-making process, then, is that sherry is fortified (and sweetened, if deemed desirable) *after* fermentation whereas port is fortified *at the height of* fermentation and while the must is still sweet.

After fermentation has been thus stopped by the added spirits, the young port is allowed to clear and is then racked into clean "pipes," which are the standard casks of the Douro district. These, unlike butts of young sherry, are kept constantly filled to the bung. In the spring the young wines are shipped downstream to the "lodges" of the Oporto shippers, for aging and manipulation. Like sherry, port is a blended wine, and there are three principal types: vintage port, ruby port, and tawny port. The distinctions need not concern us here. The point of immediate concern is that the essence of the port-making process—fortification in mid-fermentation, when the must still contains sugar —may be applied to any grapes, grown anywhere, not infrequently with interesting results and especially if the resulting sweet wine is aged for several years in small oak cooperage. The fortification must be done, however, with some precision. That is to say, the correct moment for fortification must be chosen and the correct proportion of spirit of a given strength [2] must be used.

There is a useful formula for determining the amount of fortifying brandy to add to any given must to raise its alcoholic content to a predetermined fortification point. Its use is best explained by means of a concrete example. Assume that the wine-maker starts with a must containing 24 per cent of sugar, and that fermentation reduces its sugar con-

----

[2] The amateur can of course use only tax-paid spirits for fortification; commercial wine-makers may use bonded (i.e., untaxed) spirits, provided they meet the rather complicated regulations.

tent to 10 per cent while developing an alcoholic content of 7 per cent by volume. The wine-maker wants to add enough brandy to make a port of 18 per cent alcohol. The alcoholic strength of his fortifying brandy is 70 per cent by volume; with this he wants to raise the alcoholic content of his fermenting must from 7 volume per cent to 18 volume per cent.[3] He arranges these three figures as follows:

alcoholic strength of brandy		*alcoholic strength of must*
70	*fortification point*	7
	18	

By subtracting the 18 from the 70 *crosswise* in one direction, and the 7 from the 18 in another, he gets the following answers, indicated in **boldface**.

70		7
	18	
11		**52**
gal. brandy		*gal. must*

Or, in normal language, 11 gallons of 70 per cent brandy will fortify 52 gallons of 7 per cent must to yield 63 gallons of sweet wine fortified to 18 per cent of alcohol. The amount of brandy of any given strength to add to must of any given strength to reach any required fortification point may be determined very quickly by substituting the appropriate figures.

---

[3] In using the formula the wine-maker may work either in percentage by volume or in percentage by weight, but he cannot mix the two.

CHAPTER XV

The Use of Wine

For reasons tentatively set forth in earlier chapters, Americans have never become wine-drinkers in the sense that the French and most other Europeans (including even a good many Englishmen) are. For most Americans, wine is not a familiar thing. On the contrary, it is regarded uneasily as something alien and filled with mystery; and most of the writing that is addressed to Americans on the subject of wine and its use does nothing to encourage familiarity. It manages somehow to give the impression that the use of wine is an affectation. Encountering such wine gibberish, most Americans quite sensibly turn aside with a yawn and decide to stick to their occasional highball, cocktail, and bottle of beer.

I should like, if I can, to spend these last few pages in bringing the matter of wine-drinking down out of the clouds of fancy writing and misinformation. Wine isn't anything to be afraid of or suspicious of. The use of it isn't a problem in etiquette.[1] It doesn't need any hocus-pocus. If

---

[1] Nor is it more than an insignificant element in the problem of alcoholism. The current concern in France with alcoholism is with the use

it did, there wouldn't be a liter bottle of it in the lunch basket of every Italian road-worker or farmhand, nor would the French peasant find it equally useful as a mouth wash in the morning, as a religious symbol on Sunday, as the high point of every feast, and as a component of his simple everyday supper. Wine and the vine with such people are in a manner of speaking members of the family and are so treated. The exceptional wine, like the exceptional son or daughter, yields a very special satisfaction; the ordinary wine is taken for what it is and no great demands are put upon it; the sickly wine, the problem wine, the feeble wine, may cause private sorrow, but are faithfully cared for and given the benefit of the doubt. All are members of the family. Poor vintage follows fine vintage, but both have their place in the scheme of things. Such is life! And such is the attitude toward wine and the vine in what a contemporary Frenchman has called the *"civilisation de la vigne."*

YOUNG WINE OR OLD?

The importance of age can be and usually is greatly exaggerated. True, a superior red wine or a very "big" white wine gains greatly by a few years in bottle. But many wines —in fact, most wines—are at their best when young. The

and abuse of cheap spirits and fabricated *apéritifs*, especially the untaxed *eaux de vie* produced under what we would call bootleg conditions. A recent study brings out the fact once again that the *départements* in which alcoholism is a most serious social problem are Calvados, Manche, Orne, Mayenne, Morbihan, Côtes du Nord. These are non-viticultural *départements*. Indeed, they are the *départements* in which most of France's milk and dairy products are produced.

white wines and rosés especially are quite ready to drink when they have fallen bright in the spring after vintage. A sound practice is to draw off a portion of the vintage at this time into gallon jugs for immediate use. A gallon of such wine, once opened, must be kept in the refrigerator, but there it will hold without deterioration until used up. Simply pour as needed into carafe or pitcher, putting the jug back immediately. Light young red wines are good, too, when handled this way and drunk cold. It is simply not true that red wines must always be served at "room temperature."

WHAT TEMPERATURE?

Americans, owing probably to our climate and our taste in central heating, like to drink things that are either hot or cold, but not tepid: hot coffee and tea, cold water and milk and beer and soft drinks and juices. Wine is not good when served hot, so the right way to serve it in our country is cold, or at least cool. So far as white wines and rosé are concerned, this is fairly well understood already. But the general rule does as well for all but the finest red wines. The one serious objection to the chilling of red wines is that many of them become cloudy when cold; and this is particularly true of red wines such as Bordeaux, which contain an abundance of tannin. But the American notion of "room temperature," which is to say a temperature ranging from 72° to 78° F., and even higher in the summer, is definitely wrong for red wine. The "room temperature" rule for red wines was promulgated by the English, whose room temperature is likely to be closer to 60° than to 70°. For the very finest Bordeaux and Burgundies, a serving temperature of 65° is ideal; [2] for lesser red wines a half-hour in the refrigerator, bringing down their temperature to around 55°, is a sound practice.

MANNER OF SERVICE

Be bound by no fancied notions of "correctness." Experience has led to certain conclusions regarding the service of very fine wines and very old wines. But first a word or two about the manner of serving ordinary, everyday wines.

If you serve from the bottle, pull the cork at the table. It is a pretty ceremony, and it prepares the mind for what is to come. But get yourself a decent corkscrew, something better than a ten-cent-store can-opener. If the bottle is not all drunk, put the rest of it, corked, back in the refrigerator, and have it for supper the next day. If several tail ends accumulate in the refrigerator, do not hesitate to mix them together. Often such mixtures taste better than any one of the original parts, just as beef stew frequently tastes better the second night.

If your bottles are not particularly attractive, or if your wine has developed a sediment, decant into a clear glass carafe or pitcher (but never a metal pitcher).

Do not worry overmuch about glasses. In Italy and France, stemmed glasses are seen in the better restaurants, and in private homes for gala occasions, but almost never

[2] Such wines are easily warmed a bit more in the glass, to bring out the full bouquet.

for the ordinary household service of wine. For this purpose the glasses used more or less resemble the small tumblers that every American family uses for orange juice. Use these same glasses for wine and make no apologies.

And yet for really superior wines there is much to be said for the classic stemmed wineglass. The requirements are that the glass shall display the wine to best advantage, that it shall give the wine a proper opportunity to develop its bouquet, and that it shall be large enough. The glasses, then, should not be colored, and they should be clear and

Wineglass of classic shape.

fairly thin and unfussy. As for the second requirement, there has never been an improvement over the tulip-shaped glass that is illustrated. In this the bouquet is concentrated to some extent, and the wine may be swirled around if the taster should be inclined to swirl it. There is sense, too, in the stems, for they enable one to lift the glass without smudging the bowl with fingerprints. Finally, the glass should be of ample size. In the United States, most wine-glasses are much too small; a six-ounce or better yet an eight-ounce glass of good design, if it can be found, serves well for any sort of wine, white or red, dry or sweet, still or sparkling.

Now for the question of decanting. It is entirely normal for an aged wine, especially a red wine, to throw down some sediment. If such wine is served direct from the bottle, only the first glass or two will be clear. This is likely to be true even though a wine-basket is used. The thing to do, then, is to separate wine from sediment before serving. This is done by standing up the bottle for twenty-four hours in advance of use. The sediment thus slips down the side of the bottle to the bottom. When ready, draw the cork slowly and carefully. Holding the bottle firmly in one hand, and a carafe or glass pitcher in the other, raise to a light and pour very slowly and carefully from bottle into carafe. At a given point, when most of the wine has been decanted, the sediment will be seen to begin to creep toward the mouth of the bottle. Just as it reaches the mouth, stop pouring. If this is carefully done, not more than a third of a glass of wine will be wasted, and the wine will be clear (and will also benefit by the brief airing). Put cork, carafe, *and bottle* on the table if those present are experienced wine-drinkers. They may be interested in the label, and they may wish to examine the cork. But *don't* make a fuss about all this procedure unless those present know something about wine and know what you are up to.

WHAT WINE, WHAT FOOD?

And so we come to the question of matching the wine with the food—a question that may be approached from either end. That is to say, the wine may be chosen to accompany the food, or the food to accompany the wine. Let us all, for the moment, be connoisseurs. That granted, the determining factors are of course the character of the dinner and the interests of the persons who are to sit down together. If the company is to consist of congenial people who like wine but pretend to no great knowledge of it, then the thing to do obviously is to fit the wine to the food, which is a matter of utmost simplicity. An opening of oysters, soup, or other preliminary fodder becomes something rather special with a bottle or a carafe of dry white wine. If seafood is to follow, or a casserole of chicken or something else light, more white wine is appropriate—the same wine or something better. On the other hand, food of a more hearty character—meat, a turkey or a duck, spaghetti —does better with a red wine or a rosé. (Why? Who can say? But no one who knows wine will disagree that in a carefully planned meal red wine is always best with meat and the heavier dishes whereas white wine complements, and is complemented by, the fruits of the sea and lighter fare.) If cheese is to figure later in the proceedings, more red wine is appropriate; if ice cream or lemon pie or a gooey desert, no more. For such a dinner, the wines served may receive no direct attention whatsoever; nevertheless their contribution to the dinner will be real and important.

If there is to be a gathering of people who know wine and are consciously interested, then the case is rather different. Then the wines to be served are the stars of the occasion and will be closely examined and appreciated; they are rather likely to dominate conversation at least part of the time. In that case it will be the food, not the wine, that is or should be unobtrusive. Self-assertive foods—things that are highly seasoned or of pronounced intrinsic flavor, such as peppery soups or pigs' knuckles and sauerkraut, or foods that tend to kill the character of any wine, such as egg dishes or pork chops, or foods that must be struggled with, such as steamed crabs or bony little birds—all such things as these are to be avoided on the occasion we are considering, good and nourishing as they would be at another time. By a process of elimination one arrives, for such a wine-tasting meal, at a simple menu on the bland side, of the sort that can be strung out indefinitely, and with plenty of good bread and butter and most certainly a little cheese with which to finish off the bottles. Silly? Yes, if there are people who are not interested. It is probably silly anyway, if one insists on seeing it so. Perhaps it is silly, too, to go out of one's way to hear four string players struggle through some of the quartets of Beethoven, or to attend the ballet to see some highly specialized young ladies and gentlemen prance around in black tights on the tips of their toes to the tune of a forty-piece orchestra. But, like these, a wine-tasting dinner can be fascinating and even exciting if one is properly conditioned.

Above everything, remember that the amateur wine-maker is in constant and deadly danger of being a bore, or boor. There are two reasons for this. The first is that, being a person who appreciates wine, while living in a culture that is indifferent if not downright hostile to it, he passes all too easily into a mood of righteous indignation or missionary zeal. The little lady who refuses wine because it "disagrees" with her moves him to exasperation and withering scorn and tempts him into a lecture on the therapeutic uses of wine. The highball-drinking friend who quickly disposes of his first glass of wine and cheerfully accepts a second is too easily mistaken for a potential convert ready for final exhortation. Better, far better, to talk of other things while letting the wine itself go about the subtle business of conversion. The second reason is that the wine-maker, having fought and conquered, having participated so to speak in an act of creation whereby a tub of grapes becomes a tolerable bottle of wine, makes the mistake so many young mothers make of assuming that everyone glories in an evident miracle. To all but the parents, one baby is very much like another. To all but the wine-maker, a bottle of wine is nothing more than another bottle of wine, to be enjoyed or not enjoyed as the case may be. The lady on your left does not want to know how triumph was snatched from failure by an eleventh-hour induction of malo-lactic fermentation. The gentleman across the table doesn't care whether the wine contains 5 p.p.m. of free SO_2 or 1,005. He doesn't care what the sugar content of your grapes was on the 10th of September, nor is he the least curious about the number of gallons of wine to be made in a good year from 62 vines of Seyve-Villard 14–287. If he says he is, don't believe him.

He is being only polite, and is unconsciously preparing the rupture of a beautiful friendship. When people tell you that your precious Seibel 5279 is the most delicious homemade wine they have ever tasted, accept the compliment with a courteous inclination of the head, and change the subject. When they insist that they *wish* you would tell them how you do it, under no circumstances oblige them with an explanation. If you are tempted into beginning, accept the warning glance of your wife as having been given in your best interest and taper off as swiftly as possible. Be content that your friends enjoy your wine, and let it go at that.

WINE EVERY DAY

Finally, one or two things ought to be said about *consommation*, or ordinary wine-drinking. People who use wine freely are concerned much less with fine wines than with those called ordinary. These are apt to be wines of no very pronounced character or virtue, except that of being wine, and for that reason they wear well in daily service. For the city dweller who does not make wine for his own use, the "standard" wines of California are almost inevitably the answer. He shops around until he finds one that is to his liking and then sticks to it. As often as not, it is wine that comes in a gallon jug, having been shipped out of California by tank car and bottled close to the market. Such wine is hardly more expensive than the household coffee, and if properly handled its quality need not deteriorate. Often it is not properly handled. The thing to do, if gallon wine is the choice, is to equip oneself with a few dozen used wine bottles, some fifths and some half-bottles, and to save some used wine corks that are in sound condition. When a new gallon is bought, rinse some bottles and rinse and bring to a boil in a saucepan the necessary number of used corks. Pour the wine from the jug into the bottles, using a small plastic kitchen funnel, and cork. A small hand corker like the one shown on page 115 makes this simple and easy. The whole operation can be done in ten minutes or less, and the wine will then keep indefinitely. For everyday drinking, the "standard" red wines of California wear better than the white.

As for the domestic wine-maker, he may occasionally surprise himself with a vintage of exceptional character. But this is not the rule, and the domestic wine-maker will be unwise to count on anything better than a sound *ordinaire*, at least during his novitiate.

In the wine-drinking household the choice of wine is distinctly subordinate, of course, to the choice of food. In most such homes, especially the more humble ones, there is but a single wine of consumption, usually a red. Then there is no choice at all. Choice first enters when a white wine joins the red in cellar or pantry. The plain and useful red remains, of course, the basis of the family's wine-drinking, but the white provides occasional variation. The appearance at the table of one or the other is as regular as the appearance of bread and is greeted with much the same placid satisfaction, which is to say that it is taken for granted and that it is most appreciated when, through some temporary misfortune, it is missing.

When the domestic wine-maker adds other varieties of wine to his cellar, he may begin to play about with the fitting of various wines to various foods; but this is a satisfaction distinctly secondary to that of having wine, any wine, on the table. In any case, no pretentious nonsense: the wine that tastes right in the given circumstances is the right wine to have. And anyone who follows this simple prescription will find that plain food is capable of the most surprising exaltation by good domestic wines. Before long, perhaps, he will begin to understand the wisdom of the venerable gentleman who explained his vigorous old age by saying that every day since he could remember he had drunk a bottle of wine, except when he did not feel well, and then he had drunk two.

Appendix A

GRAPES FOR TABLE WINES

1: CALIFORNIA WINE GRAPES, RED

THE CHOICE of red-wine grapes for California narrows down to less than two dozen. This list includes the favored heavy producers of ordinary wines as well as the varieties capable of producing superior wines.

Following the name of each variety a number will be found in parentheses. This is the American-Winkler rating [1] of the variety's value in terms of wine quality, on a scale of 0 to 100. An asterisk (*) indicates a shipping variety usually available in Eastern markets.

Alicante Bouschet (40). Widely planted, producing a coarse wine, deeply colored, of ordinary quality, which has become almost a drug on the market. It dominates shipments to the Eastern markets. Though its intense color offers certain advantages, it should be avoided unless there is nothing better.

Barbera (78). From the Italian Piedmont, producing an agreeably rough and deeply colored wine with a characteristic aroma, ages well. It does well in the hotter parts of California.

Cabernet Sauvignon (98). Best of the California red-wine grapes so far as quality is concerned, being also the dominant French Bordeaux grape. A moderate producer, especially well adapted to the Napa and Sonoma valleys.

---

[1] See M. A. Amerine and A. J. Winkler: *Composition and Quality of Musts and Wines of California Grapes*, (Hilgardia, 1944) and *California Wine Grapes*, (Exp. Station Bulletin 794, 1963).

Carignane (57). A grape of great antiquity, if not of noble lineage, and of Spanish origin. In the north-coast counties of California it produces a well-colored wine of moderate acidity, good balance, and neutral flavor. Grown in the hot Central Valley, its wine is extremely coarse. Like the Alicante Bouschet, it is shipped east in large quantities.

Charbono (59). A secondary variety that does fairly well in the cool coastal areas of California, producing a wine somewhat above the average.

Gamay (70). The grape of the Beaujolais region in France and to a lesser extent of the Burgundy region. There are small plantings of it in California, where, in the cooler areas, it can produce wine of distinctly superior quality. Also excellent for rosé wine. Not all of the vines called Gamay in California are the true Gamay of Beaujolais.

Grand Noir (46). Near relative of the Alicante Bouschet. Wine-makers looking for quality will steer clear of it.

Grenache (82). Does well in both the cool and the hot areas. In the cool areas it yields a dry red wine, rather short of color but of good quality, and is used a good deal for making rosé. In the warm areas it develops extremely high sugar content and becomes suitable for making sweet red wine of superior quality. The French Banyuls, resembling port, is made from the Grenache grapes; on the other hand the best-known French rosé, Tavel, is also made of the Grenache.

Grignolino (79). Another variety from the Italian Piedmont producing a highly characteristic wine of an orange-pink tint, with a special aroma and an exceptionally high tannin content.

Gros Manzenc (72). Better than average quality, resembling Barbera. Does well in all but the hottest areas.

Mondeuse (67). One of the older varieties from southern France. Its wine has character when grown in the cooler parts and is usually blended with more neutral wine. It makes good

ordinary wine when grown in the hot central valleys.
Petite Sirah (71). This variety from the Rhone Valley of
France produces wine in the middle range of quality—distinctly better than the average, but inferior to Cabernet Sauvignon
and Gamay. When young, the wine is deeply colored and
astringent, with a pronounced aroma. It requires aging in cooperage, and should have aging in bottle also—after which it resembles Côtes du Rhône.

Pinot Noir (92). The source of the best Burgundies in
France, but it has been far from satisfactory in California.
Culturally, it has many drawbacks; and though it has occasionally produced wines of very fine quality, normally its wines are
mediocre—mere caricatures of true Burgundy.[2]

Refosco (65). Still another Italian, producing a good "firm"
wine, moderately productive. Indistinguishable from Mondeuse.

Ruby Cabernet. A cross between Cabernet Sauvignon and
Carignane. Considerable Cabernet character, yet thanks to the
Carignane parentage it adapts well to the Central Valley and
other hot-country areas. Variety of choice for these areas and
being heavily planted. Inexplicably, it does better in the East
than Cabernet Sauvignon.

Sangioveto (68). A Tuscan grape, the principal ingredient of
true Chianti. (The Chianti-type California wines generally
available on the market contain none of it.) Its wine is well-
balanced, tart, a little short of color, and agreeably spicy in
aroma. Very little of it is planted in California.

Tannat (69). From southwestern France, where in centuries
past its wine was shipped down the Garonne to Bordeaux to
strengthen and enrich the Bordeaux wines in poor years. It is
full-bodied, well-balanced, altogether desirable, especially
when grown in the north-coast areas. Why it has not been
more widely planted is a mystery, for it deserves to be.

[2] There are certain subvarieties of Pinot grown in California which
are easier to handle in the winery but make wine hardly distinguishable
from any other good solid California red wine.

Valdepeñas (58). Its wine is somewhat better than ordinary; the vine is adapted to the Central Valley.

Zinfandel (67). California's leading red-wine variety, of unknown but presumably Hungarian origin. A heavy producer, and though it has certain cultural defects, it is one of the most satisfactory all-around grapes for California. There is a vast difference, however, between a well-balanced and agreeably aromatic Zinfandel from the north-coast counties and the coarse, heavy, low-acid Zinfandels from the Central Valley. Shipped east in large quantities, but most of those which are shipped are from the Central Valley vineyards.

2: CALIFORNIA WINE GRAPES, WHITE

California, like the Mediterranean lands, is primarily red-wine country, and in practice this means that good California red-wine grapes are easier to come by than good California white-wine grapes. This is especially true, of course, in the Eastern market. The number behind each name indicates relative wine quality on a scale of 0 to 100, and an asterisk (*) indicates a shipping variety.

Burger (61). One of the most widely grown varieties. It is presumed to be of German origin, though its wine is not at all like the German wines. A heavy producer. Its wine, though agreeable when made from grapes that are not too ripe, is nondescript.

Chardonnay (92). This, the Burgundy white-wine grape, produces some of the best of the California white wine, when picked promptly. It is a moderate producer, well adapted only to the cooler areas. It is being heavily planted now.

Chenin Blanc. Often wrongly called White Pinot in California. A good producer, and wine is more fruity than most California whites. It is being heavily planted.

246

Folle Blanche (69). A variety from the cognac region of France. In California it is used not for brandy-making but for making white table wine of better than average quality, and also in the blends for sparkling wine. It is much more readily available than, say, Chardonnay.

French Colombard (67). *Synonyms,* West's White Prolific and Winkler. Its naturally high acidity makes it useful in hot regions and for brandy. The name Colombard is sometimes wrongly applied to Sauvignon Vert.

Gray Riesling (47). The true name of this grape is Chauché Gris. It is not a true Riesling. Its wine is pleasant, soft, and usually a bit short of acidity.

Green Hungarian (51). Of unknown origin and widely planted in California. Culturally, it is a good variety, but its wine is nondescript.

*Palomino (48). More familiar in California as the Napa Golden Chasselas, though it is not a Chasselas variety at all. It is a very fine sherry grape, and is now being used in California for this purpose. For years it was the principal ingredient of much California "Chablis," though the character of its wine does not remotely resemble Chablis. To be avoided for table wine.

Pinot Blanc (83). First cousin to the Chardonnay. Its best wines approximate those of the Chardonnay and show the specific characteristics of the better French white Burgundies as to aroma, color, and flavor. It is a better producer, and behaves better during fermentation, than Chardonnay. Not much of it is planted.

Peverella (77). From the Italian Tyrol. Its wine is better than average when made from grapes grown in the cool areas.

Red Traminer (81). Known as Gewurz Traminer, the variety from which the sumptuous Traminer wines of Alsace are made. The characteristic aroma comes over in California also, though in exaggerated form. One of the better varieties for the cool regions.

Sauvignon Blanc (78). From the Sauternes district of France, where it contributes high alcohol and a rather pronounced aroma to the traditional Sauternes blend. It serves the same purpose in California, and is also used by some producers, by itself, to produce a wine of distinct character. To my mind a well made dry Sauvignon Blanc is often superior to most California Chardonnays.

Sauvignon Vert (48). Mentioned only as a warning. Inferior to Sauvignon Blanc in all respects except its productivity, and unfortunately much more widely grown.

Sémillon (85). The principal grape of the Sauternes district of France, and the most widely planted of the superior white-wine varieties in California. For dry wine, it does best in the cool to moderate areas of California, and should be picked before it is too ripe. At its best, California Sémillon compares with good dry Graves.

Sylvaner (85). Second in popularity to the Riesling in the vineyards of Germany, Alsace, and central Europe, being more productive, and capable of producing a wine which, though inferior to the best Riesling, is well above average in quality. It does reasonably well in the cooler parts of California, despite a tendency to mildew and rot. For best wine quality under California conditions it should be picked promptly. Sometimes called Franken Riesling.

*Thompson Seedless (no rating). Also named Sultanina. The most important commercial variety in California, grown primarily for shipping as fresh fruit and for the production of seedless raisins. It is a triple-threat grape, however, the surplus always going to the wineries. Its wine is almost completely neutral in character, and if table wine is made of it, it should be blended with a wine having some trace of personality. Men-

tioned here only because in many Eastern markets it is the only California grape at all suitable for white wine.

White Riesling (88). This is the true Riesling from which the most famous Rhine wines and Moselles are made exclusively. One may not expect to produce wines of comparable quality in California, owing to the extreme climatic differences, yet the best California Riesling, grown in the cooler areas, can be very good.

3 : OLD EASTERN WINE GRAPES, RED

Eastern winegrowers have their choice between the old standard native varieties, of which the Concord is the most familiar, and the new hybrids. The old standard varieties all have special and pronounced aromas and flavors, which distinguish their wines sharply from the wines of Europe (or of California).

Bacchus. An old cross between *Vitis riparia* and *V. labrusca*, in which the foxy flavor is relatively slight, sugar content is adequate, and acidity is always high.

Clevener. Another riparia-labrusca hybrid of characteristics somewhat similar to Bacchus, now very little grown. No relation to the Alsatian Klevner.

Clinton. A red riparia-labrusca hybrid hard to come by now and hardly worth the search.

Cynthiana. See Norton.

Delicatessen. A complex hybrid originated in Texas by T. V. Munson. Intense color, so that it is useful in blending, and an agreeable, raspberry-like, entirely non-foxy aroma. Sugar content is always low.

Eumelan. An old variety with grave cultural defects, a poor producer, and with little to commend it for wine.

Ives. A riparia-labrusca hybrid in which the labrusca and

hence the foxiness predominate. One of the favorites in the days before prohibition, it is still grown to a limited extent in parts of Ohio and New York mainly for its color.

Lenoir. Rarely grown. One of the American varieties that the French accepted and still use to a limited extent.

Norton. The best of the old native red varieties, once grown a good deal in Virginia and Missouri. It has adequate sugar content and high acidity, and is not foxy. It makes a quite acceptable wine.

4: NEW EASTERN WINE GRAPES, RED

When it comes to the new hybrids, the wine-maker is confronted with a situation not unlike that confronted by the public in the early days of the motorcar, when there were hundreds of makes and models to choose from and the problems of engineering, style, and manufacture had not yet been fully worked out. In France the situation regarding the hybrids, as we have seen already, is beginning to settle down; certain of them have made permanent places for themselves in French viticulture. In this country the hybrids have been grown for less than a quarter of a century, which in a matter like adapting grape varieties is a short time. Which varieties do best in which areas is a question that is far from settled; and in addition many of the hybrids, especially the more recent ones, have hardly been tested at all.[3]

The best way of introducing the question is, perhaps, to introduce the hybrids by groups.

Baco Hybrids. Maurice Baco, living not far from Bordeaux, made many thousands of seedlings, but narrowed them down

[3] For a detailed discussion and description of these varieties see Philip M. Wagner: *A Wine-Grower's Guide*, (New York: Alfred A. Knopf; 1969).

to no more than a half dozen. Of these, only two or three have stood the test of time. The only one now being grown in the United States is Baco No. 1, an extremely vigorous and moderately productive variety yielding a wine which, with age, becomes superior, with some resemblance to the red wines of Bordeaux.

Couderc Hybrids. Couderc was one of the earliest of French hybridizers. His most successful hybrids today find their use in France and other vinifera-growing regions as rootstocks. Of his red-wine hybrids, only two are grown to any great extent today—Couderc 4401, an early ripening, moderately productive variety, very hardy, producing a wine of only passable quality; and Couderc 7120, a late-ripening variety grown considerably in southern France for *ordinaire* and not grown at all in this country.

Burdin Hybrids. The Burdins are contemporary hybridizers and are still at work. They are breeding for quality, with the primary aim of developing hybrids whose wine resembles that of the Pinot Noir and the Gamay. Many of their hybrids have inherited cultural defects from the vinifera. But in their later hybrids these defects have been overcome. Certain varieties are culturally satisfactory and yield wine virtually identical with Gamay Beaujolais.

Galibert Hybrids. The Galibert hybrids have only recently been introduced in France. They are bred primarily for the long-season conditions of southern France, and are not likely to have very wide adaptation in the United States.

Joannès-Seyve Hybrids. Joannès-Seyve is another contemporary hybridizer, and like Galibert is chiefly interested in producing hybrids for the Midi. But S.V. 26–205 has proved widely adaptable in Europe, and is doing well here. It is highly productive and its wine is excellent.

Kuhlmann Hybrids. This family of varieties has been bred primarily for Alsatian conditions, and includes several varieties promising for Northeastern American conditions both as to hardiness and vigor and as to wine quality. The most promising are those known as Maréchal Foch, Maréchal Joffre, and Léon Millot.

Landot Hybrids. Landot is another contemporary seeking to breed varieties resembling the Gamay and the Pinot Noir. Many of his varieties have proved culturally defective. Landot 204 is a *teinturier.* Landot 244, ripening early, producing only moderately, yields a superior wine resembling Beaujolais. Landot 2283 shows promise, as do L. 3381 and L. 4511.

Ravat Hybrids. Ravat, who died not many years ago, was another of the French hybridizers interested chiefly in wine quality. His work is now being carried on by his son-in-law Jean Tissier. The best of the red Ravat hybrids is Ravat 262, again somewhat resembling a Beaujolais.

Seibel Hybrids. Seibel, another of the early French hybridizers, was by far the most prolific and successful in his productions, up until recent years. He released hundreds of varieties, of greatly varying characteristics both culturally and in terms of quality. To list them all is out of the question.[4] There follow extremely brief descriptions of those which have been most widely tested in the United States and are currently the most popular. Seibel 1000, early, hardy, a capricious producer of neutral wine of good quality lacking in color; Seibel 4643, a heavy producer of heavy-bodied, neutral wine, medium early, adapted to dry conditions; Seibel 5455, early midseason, neutral aroma, well-balanced wine; Seibel 7053, early midseason, heaviest producer of all, well-balanced wine of good quality, rather weak vine; Seibel 8357, a *teinturier* of great value in blending because of its intense color and neutral flavor; Seibel 10878, mid-early, grown a good deal on the wrong side of the road in French Burgundy, wine of good quality with an agreeable aroma; Seibel 13053, earliest of all, hardy, heavy producer,

[4] See Wagner, op. cit.

vigorous, wine has rather weak color and is best when made as a rosé; Seibel 13666, yielding wine of deep color and some kinship to Beaujolais; Seibel 14596, vigorous and productive.

Seyve-Villard Hybrids. Seyve-Villard, a contemporary, is (so far) much the most successful producer of hybrids for hot climates, and has in addition produced some hardy hybrids adaptable to short-season conditions. His most successful red-wine hybrids are the following: Seyve-Villard 5247, early ripening, vigorous, and productive, big crops, wine neutral and rather light in color; Seyve-Villard 12417, midseason, ordinary wine, adapted only to hot conditions; Seyve-Villard 13359, huge producer, wine soft, well-colored, agreeable; Scyve-Villard 18283, early midseason, vigorous vine, heavy producer, good *ordinaire;* Seyve-Villard 18315, early midseason, heavy producer, rather weak vine, good quality; Seyve-Villard 18402, early midseason, heavy producer, succeeds only under hot conditions and should usually be grafted; Seyve-Villard 23657, early midseason, vigorous vine, wine distinctly superior to the two preceding.

5 : OLD EASTERN WINE GRAPES, WHITE

The wine quality of the old standard Eastern white-wine grapes is very much superior to that of the old red-wine grapes. Several of those mentioned below clearly have a permanent place in Eastern viticulture.

Catawba. A serviceable variety still grown in substantial quantities, particularly in the Finger Lakes district of New York and in the winegrowing district around Sandusky, Ohio. It is highly foxy when tasted as fresh fruit, but the foxiness is much less conspicuous if the must is carefully pressed from the skins. Adequate sugar content and high acid in most areas. Its wine has a pronounced character—too pronounced for some—

and is the basis of most Eastern champagne blends. The defect of the variety is that it ripens quite late.

Delaware. This is generally conceded to be the best of the native white-wine grapes and is still grown in substantial quantities in the Finger Lakes region. Under normal conditions it is a relatively light bearer, though very regular. High sugar and moderate acidity. The wine is excellent unblended, with a delicate and distinct aroma entirely its own, and still better when blended with a more neutral wine. Much used in Eastern champagne blends.

Diamond. One of the best of the older table grapes, but too foxy for the production of good wine. In the East it is sometimes used in blends with neutral California wines.

Dutchess. An old hybrid, not very hardy and not very productive, still grown in small quantities and used in champagne blends.

Elvira. A cross between riparia and labrusca, ripening very early and yielding a wine of ordinary quality. It has very low sugar content.

Missouri Riesling. The name is misleading, because this riparia-vinifera hybrid has no Riesling blood in it at all. Wine slightly better than average quality, but of no very great interest.

Noah. This old hybrid bears the curious distinction of being better known to European winegrowers than to those of the United States. Being rustic and a good producer, it is still grown a good deal in France and elsewhere for family wine of mediocre quality.

6: NEW EASTERN WINE GRAPES, WHITE

What was said about the new hybrids in relation to red wine applies to the new French hybrids in relation to white wines.

Many of these new and promising varieties have been introduced into the United States; and they are being grown and tried out for wine under the most varied conditions. Results so far offer great promise for the future, as witness the fact that the leading Eastern wineries are now making extensive plantings of some of them. It is still best, however, to discuss them in groups without making final and positive recommendations.

Baco Hybrids. Two of these have been introduced, Baco 22-A, which has made a reputation in southwestern France for the production of ordinary table wine and for the production of armagnac; and an early-ripening variety, Tôtmur, which has not yet been tested for wine quality.

Couderc Hybrids. The variety Couderc 13, grown a good deal in southern France, appears to be finding congenial conditions in the Southern United States. Couderc 299–35 is a large-berried muscat suitable for table or for imparting muscat aroma to blends.

Burdin Hybrids. There exists a great array of these, about which, so far, it is possible to say only that Burdin 4672 and Burdin 5201 behave well and make wine recalling Alsace.

Galibert Hybrids. These recent productions are interesting because a number of them contain the blood of Sémillon, the Sauternes grape. Very little can be said so far about their adaptation to American conditions.

Landot Hybrids. The most promising appear to be Landot 2281 and Landot 2282, though neither appears to be sufficiently vigorous to be grown ungrafted.

New York State Hybrids. A number of our state experiment stations have grape-breeding programs. Most of these are directed to the production of new table varieties, with, so far, ambiguous results. A notable exception is the grape-breeding program of the New York State Experiment Station at Geneva, initiated by the late Dr. U. P. Hedrick and carried on in the competent hands of Dr. Richard Wellington. New table grapes hold primary interest in this program, and in this field the results have been notably successful. Hector, Ontario, Ripley, Seneca, and Van Buren, for example, have already found places for themselves in both amateur and commercial vineyards, and there exist several seedless varieties, notably Interlaken, Himrod and Romulus, which have a promising future. Winegrowing requirements also have a part in this program; and if progress has been slower, it is only because the task of developing wine varieties superior to the French hybrids already available is intrinsically more difficult. Yet Hector, Ripley, and Van Buren are not without value to the wine-maker. And the variety Steuben, a beautiful lavender grape, which is also delicious for eating, is sometimes used for the production of a white wine distantly recalling the white wines of Alsace. More will be heard of this station's productions in the years to come.

Ravat Hybrids. Of these, Ravat 6 stands out as best in its wine character. In the Beaujolais district, the best wines of this variety strongly resemble the celebrated Pouilly. Its wine, under appropriate soil and climatic conditions, has a distinct resemblance to that of the Chardonnay, which indeed is one of its parents. Under American conditions its hardiness is very doubtful. A more hardy one is Ravat 51; an earlier, Ravat 578.

Seibel Hybrids. Among the Seibel productions, as with the red-wine hybrids, are to be found the varieties that have had the most thorough testing so far under American conditions and about which it is possible to speak with confidence. Among those which have proved themselves in one part of the country or another are the following: Seibel 4986, midseason, superior wine of good acidity; Seibel 5279, very early, wine somewhat resembling the Alsatian wines, with good sugar and acid balance, vine hardy and productive; Seibel 10868, early midseason, very hardy and disease-resistant, wine resembling that of Seibel 4986; Seibel 9110, early midseason, fruit especially beautiful, useful either as fresh fruit or for the production of an agreeably perfumed wine; Seibel 13047, early, huge producer, ripening between Seibel 5279 and Seibel 9110, wine neutral, soft, with good body, admirable for blending.[5]

Seyve-Villard Hybrids. A number of these have been rather thoroughly tested in the United States, among them: Seyve-Villard 5276, early, huge producer, of medium vigor, extremely "clean" wine resembling the French Muscadet; Seyve-Villard 12303, late midseason, for Southern areas; Seyve-Villard 12309, late midseason, wine quality somewhat superior to Seyve-Villard 12303, good producer; Seyve-Villard 12375, midseason, vine of great vigor and productivity, a warm-area counterpart to Seyve-Villard 5276; Seyve-Villard 14287, early, vine of medium vigor but productive, a true Muscat suitable for either dry, still, or sparkling Muscat-type wine, or for sweet wine of the type known as Muscatel.[6]

Vidal Hybrids. This hybridizer has labored for many years to find a variety which will produce a cognac equal to that distilled from the Folle Blanche, which is terribly susceptible to the mildew diseases in the Charente. One in particular, Vidal 256, has proved admirable in all respects under eastern American conditions for the production of a crisp white wine of the Muscadet type. His other hybrids have not so far been tested here.

[5] The above are only the most widely grown. Other white-wine Seibels that deserve mention are Seibel 5409, Seibel 11803, Seibel 14514, and Seibel 15051.

[6] Certain other numbers, less thoroughly tested, deserve mention, notably: Seyve-Villard 12481, Seyve-Villard 20365, Seyve-Villard 20366, Seyve-Villard 20473 (another Muscat), Seyve-Villard 23410, Seyve-Villard 23501, and Seyve-Villard 3056.

Appendix B

CONVERSION TABLES

VOLUME
liter(s)

Hectoliter (hl.)	100	26.42	gal.
Decaliter (dcl.)	10	2.64	gal.
Liter (l.)	1	1.0567	qt.
Centiliter (cl.)	0.01	0.338	fl. oz.
Milliter (ml.)	0.001		
1 qt.	0.9463		
1 gal.	3.785		

WEIGHT
gram(s)

Kilogram (kg.)	1,000	2.204	lb.
Hectogram (hg.)	100	3.527	oz.
Decagram (dkg.)	10	0.353	oz.
Gram (gm.)	1	15.432	grains
Decigram (dg.)	0.1	1.543	grains
Centigram (cg.)	0.01		
* Milligram (mg.)	0.001		
1 gr.	0.0648		
1 oz.	28.3495		
1 lb.	453.59		

* 1 mg. = one millionth of a liter of water, hence 1 part-per-million (p.p.m.).

Appendix B

TEMPERATURE

CENTIGRADE	FAHRENHEIT
0	32
5	41
10	50
15	59
20	68
25	77
30	86
35	95
40	104
45	113
50	122
55	131
60	140
65	149
70	158
75	167
80	176
85	185
90	194
95	203
100	212

Degree centigrade = $\frac{5}{9}$ of degree Fahrenheit — 32
Degree Fahrenheit = $\frac{9}{5}$ of degree centigrade + 32

SO₂ EQUIVALENTS

To obtain parts per million (p.p.m.), or milligrams per liter, of SO₂ in 1,000 liters of must or wine	Sulphur pastilles burned in containers * gm.	Liquefied SO₂ † gm.	Potassium meta-bisulphite ‡ gm.
10	5	10	20
15	7.5	15	30
20	10	20	40
25	12.5	25	50
30	15	30	60
35	17.5	35	70
40	20	40	80
45	22.5	45	90
50	25	50	100
55	27.5	55	110
60	30	60	120
65	32.5	65	130
70	35	70	140
75		75	150
100		100	200
125		125	250
150		150	300
175		175	350
200		200	400
250		250	500
300		300	600
350		350	700

* Approximate only. Pastilles are available in sizes 2.5 gm. up.
† Introduced in a 5 per cent aqueous solution ordinarily.
‡ When dissolved, potassium metabisulphite yields half its weight of SO₂.

Bibliography

INTERNAL REVENUE SERVICE: *Wine, Publication 146* (being Part 240 of Title 26, Code of Federal Regulations). Washington: U.S. Government Printing Office, 1970. Price: 55 cents. (Official ground rules for the production of wine in the United States.)

AKENHEAD, D.: *Viticultural Research.* London: H.M. Stationery Office; 1928.

ALLEN, H. WARNER: *The Romance of Wine.* New York: Dutton; 1932.

——: *Natural Red Wines.* London: Constable; 1952.

——: *White Wines and Cognac.* London: Constable; 1952.

AMERINE, MAYNARD A., BERG., H. W., and CRUESS, W. V.: *The Technology of Wine Making.* Westport: Avi; 1967.

AMERINE, MAYNARD A., and JOSLYN, M. A.: *Table Wines, the Technology of Their Production in California.* Berkeley: University of California; 2nd ed., 1969.

—— and WHEELER, LOUISE, B.: *A Check List of Books and Pamphlets on Grapes and Wine, 1938–1948.* Berkeley: University of California; 1951.

—— and WINKLER, A. J.: *California Wine Grapes.* California Ext. Bulletin 794; 1963. (Basic recommendations on which grapes for which districts.)

BAYNES, K., and SCOTT, J. M.: *Vineyards of France.* London: Hodder & Stoughton; 1950. (Charming picture book.)

BENVEGNIN, L., CAPT. E., and PIGUET, G.: *Traité de vinification.* Lausanne: Payot; 1947.

CAROSSO, V. P.: *The California Wine Industry, 1830–1895.* Berkeley: University of California; 1951.

CATO THE CENSOR (tr. Brehaut, E.): *De agricultura.* New York: Columbia University Press; 1933.

CHAMBERLAIN, SAMUEL: *Bouquet de France, an Epicure's Tour of French Provinces* New York: Gourmet; 1952.

CHANCRIN, E.: *Le Vin.* Paris: Hachette; n.d.

CHAPPAZ, GEORGES: *Le Vignoble et le vin de Champagne.* Paris: Larmat; 1951. (Best contemporary treatise.)

COCKS, CH., and FERET, ED.: *Bordeaux et ses vins.* 12th ed. Bordeaux: Feret et Fils; 1969. (Exhaustive directory of Bordeaux wine-producers.)

DUJARDIN-SALLERON: *Notice sur les Instruments de Précision appliqués à l'Œnologie.* 6th ed., Paris.

FABRE, J. H.: *Traité encyclopédique des vins.* 3 vols. Paris, 1929. Alger, 1945, 1946.

FORBES, PATRICK: *Champagne, The Wine, the Land and the People.* New York: Reynal; 1967.

GÉNEVOIS, L., and RIBÉREAU-GAYON, J.: *Le Vin.* Paris: Hermann; 1947.

HARASZTHY, A.: *Grape Culture, Wines and Wine Making.* New York: Harper; 1862.

HEDRICK, U. P.: *The Grapes of New York.* Albany: State of New York; 1908.

——: *A History of Horticulture in America to 1860.* New York: Oxford; 1950.

—— *Manual of American Grape Growing.* New York: Macmillan; 1924.

HILGARD, E. W.: *Reports of Experiments on Methods of Fermentation.* Sacramento: University of California; 1888.

——: *Report on Viticultural Work, being a Part of the Report of the Regents of the University.* Sacramento, 1882. (Also reports in subsequent years.)

HUSMANN, GEORGE: *American Grape Growing and Wine Making.* New York: Orange, Judd; 1895.

JACQUELIN, LOUIS, and FOULAIN, RENÉ: *The Wines and Vineyards of France.* New York: Putnam; 1962. (Covers France district by district and even vineyard by vineyard.)

JOSLYN, M. A., and AMERINE, MAYNARD A.: *Dessert, Appetizer and Related Flavored Wines.* Berkeley: University of California; 1964.

LAFFORGUE, GERMAIN: *Le Vignoble Girondin.* Paris: Larmat; 1947. (Best contemporary work.)

LARMAT, LOUIS: *Atlas de la France Vinicole.* 6 vols. Paris: Larmat; 1941–7. (Detailed and beautifully printed maps of the principal winegrowing regions of France, with accompanying descriptive material and excerpts from the applicable parts of the law of *appellations d'origine.*)

LICHINE, ALEXIS: *Wines of France.* New York: Knopf; 5th ed., 1969.

—— et al.: *Alexis Lichine's Encyclopedia of Wines and Spirits.* New York: Knopf; 1967.

MARRÈS, PAUL: *La Vigne et le Vin en France.* Paris: Colin; 1950. (Best brief handbook.)

MELVILLE, JOHN: *Guide to California Wines.* San Carlos: Nourse; 3rd ed., 1968.

PACOTTET, PAUL: *Vinification.* Paris: Baillière; 1925.

—— and GUITTONNEAU, L.: *Vins de Champagne et vins mousseux.* Paris: Baillière; 1930.

RODIER, CAMILLE: *Le Vin de Bourgogne.* 3rd ed. Dijon: Damidot; 1950. (Best general work on this region.)

RIBÉREAU-GAYON, J., and PEYNAUD, E.: *Analyse et contrôle des vins.* Paris: Librairie Polytechnique; 1947.

—— and ——: *Traité d'Œnologie.* 2 vols. Paris: Béranger; 1964, 1966.

RUDD, HUGH R.: *Hocks & Moselles.* London: Constable; 1935.

SCHOONMAKER, FRANK: *Encyclopedia of Wine.* New York: Hastings House; 1964.

SEBASTIAN, V.: *Traité pratique de la preparation des vins de luxe.* Montpellier, 1909.

SHAND, P. MORTON: *A Book of French Wines.* New York: Knopf; 1928, rev. 1960.

SHAND, P. MORTON: *A Book of Other Wines than French.* New York: Knopf; 1929.

SILORET, G.: *Le Vin.* Paris: Hachette; 1963.

SIMON, ANDRÉ L.: *The Blood of the Grape.* London: Duckworth; 1920.

——: *Bibliographia Bacchica.* 2 vols. London, 1935.

STERN, G. B.: *Bouquet.* New York: Knopf; 1927.

TCHELISTCHEFF, ANDRÉ, and GRAFF, R. H.: "The Production and Aging of Wine in Small Oak Cooperage." *Wines & Vines,* Vol. 50, No. 5 (May 1969). (Best discussion in English.)

THUDICHUM, J. L. W., and DUPRÉ, A.: *A Treatise on the Origin, Nature and Varieties of Wine.* London, 1872.

VENTRE, JULES: *Traité de vinification pratique et rationelle.* 3 vols. Montpellier: Coulet; 1930–1.

VIZETELLY, HENRY: *A History of Champagne.* London: Sotheran; 1882.

WAGNER, PHILIP M.: *A Wine-Grower's Guide.* New York, 1969. (Emphasis on grape-growing rather than wine-making, with detailed discussion of varieties and cultural methods.)

WEINMANN, J.: *Manuel du travail vins mousseux.* Épernay, 1929.

WILEY, H. W.: *American Wines at the Paris Exposition of 1900.* Washington, 1903.

Index

(Names of grape species and varieties are printed in *italics*)

i

Index

Index

Index

Index

Index

A NOTE ON THE TYPE

The text of this book was set on the Linotype in JANSON, *a recutting made direct from the type cast from matrices made by Anton Janson. Whether or not Janson was of Dutch ancestry is not known, but it is known that he purchased a foundry and was a practicing type-founder in Leipzig during the years 1600 to 1687. Janson's first specimen sheet was issued in 1675. His successor issued a specimen sheet showing all of the Janson types in 1689.*

His type is an excellent example of the influential and sturdy Dutch types that prevailed in England prior to the development by William Caslon of his own incomparable designs, which he evolved from these Dutch faces. The Dutch in their turn had been influenced by Garamond in France. The general tone of Janson, however, is darker than Garamond and has a sturdiness and substance quite different from its predecessors. It is a highly legible type, and its individual letters have a pleasing variety of design. Its heavy and light strokes make it sharp and clear, and the full-page effect is characterful and harmonious.